Dear Parent,

Educating your child is one of the most important things you will ever do! But many times, we as parents have difficulty knowing how to teach our children. What techniques should we use? What skills are most important? How much time should we spend each day? **The 30-Minute-A-Day Learning System** is designed to help you answer these questions and to help keep your child learning and growing every day.

Designed by elementary and preschool teachers, this series will introduce or review the basic skills for a grade level in simple, easy lessons that your child can understand. In addition, each lesson features an Introduction page to tell you what your child will be learning about, and a unique Review and Assessment page that will help you determine if your child is understanding a concept. These pages also offer suggestions for other activities that will reinforce and expand the skills taught in each section.

By spending just 30 minutes with your child each day, you will give your child an advantage in school and in life.

How to use this book:

In order to maximize your child's learning potential, follow these simple steps below as you use your 30-Minute-A-Day Learning System:

- Create a quiet and comfortable work area.
- Gather all necessary materials for the lesson (pencils, markers, crayons, etc.) prior to starting.
- Work only one lesson a day (it should take 30 minutes or less).
- Do the lessons in the order presented. The lessons build on each other, and doing them out of order could confuse your child.
- Review each lesson after your child completes it. Determine in which areas your child excelled and which areas need more work.
- Praise success.
- Always help your child correct mistakes in a positive way-making mistakes is a part of learning.
- The Assessment page at the end of each lesson has a list of other activities that will reinforce or expand the lesson learned by using your child's own environment.

By completing these daily lessons, your child will begin to understand basic concepts. With the additional activities introduced on the Assessment pages, your child will see how these skills relate to everyday life. By combining these two concepts, you will be preparing your child for success in current and future learning!

Sincerely,

Your friends at Brighter Minds

Brighter Minds
Children's Publishing™
www.brightermindspublishing.com

Table of Contents

Chapter 1

Today's lesson will be lots of fun as we join Paige and Bogart as they investigate a mysterious island!

While they explore, you will have a good time learning how to write:
- Letters with curves
- Letters with lines
- Numbers

Now let's see what's going on at the island!

Writing the Alphabet

Trace and then write the uppercase letter **C** and the lowercase letter **c**.

cat

Cookie

Candy

The letter **C** is like part of a **c**ircle!

Writing the Alphabet

Trace and then write the uppercase letter **I** and the lowercase letter **i**.

ice cream

igloo

dig

Pig

Do you like **ice cream?**

Writing Numbers

Trace each number.
Then write each number.

Try to write each number two times.

16 16 16 16 16 16 16

17 17 17 17 17 17 17

18 18 18

19 19 19

20 20 20 20

Counting from 1 to 20

Connect the dots. Start at 1.

Count from 1 to 20. Do not skip any numbers.

What a wonderful whale!

Picturing Things

Write numbers from 0 to 10 with straight and curved

Straight lines look like this:
_____

Curved lines look like this:
‿‿‿‿‿

Numbers with straight lines

1 4 7

Numbers with curved lines

0 3 6

8

Numbers with both straight and curved lines

2 5 9

10

Numbers are fun to write!

Assessment

Chapter 1 Review

Your child studied uppercase and lowercase letters and basic number writing in this chapter.

Your child learned how to:
- Write uppercase and lowercase letters.
- Write numbers.

To review what your child has learned, do the activities below. If your child is having difficulty in any of the following areas, go back and review the pages with him or her. You can also review and reinforce the skills in this section with the additional activities listed below.

1. Have your child trace the pattern of upper and lowercase letters.

C   c   C   c   I   i   I   i   C   I   c   i   C   I   c   i

2. Ask your child to fill in the missing numbers.

1   __   3   4   5   __   7   __   9   10

3. Tell your child to circle the numbers that have curved lines.

0   1   3   4   6   7   8

Additional Activities

Below are some interactive ways you and your child can review what you have worked on in this chapter. These activities will reinforce the skills your child studied on the previous pages.

1. Use clay or dough to form letters and numbers.
2. Help your child cut uppercase and lowercase letters out of a newspaper or magazine. Paste them on a sheet of paper to spell the names of family members.
3. The next time you're at a park or playground, have your child trace numbers in the sandbox.

Chapter 2

Today's lesson will be lots of fun as we join Marco and Bogart while they play and nap on the beach!

While Marco throws a beach ball, you will have a good time learning:
- Letters with lines
- Beginning sounds
- Numbers 1-20

Now let's see what's going on at the beach!

Writing the Alphabet

Trace and write the uppercase letter **K** and the lowercase letter **k**. Then trace and write the uppercase letter **L** and the lowercase letter **l**.

key

lock
love

You are writing two letters! Terrific!

Beginning Sounds: k

Color the pictures that begin with the same sound as **kite.**

kite

Do you hear the **k** sound at the beginning of the word **kite?**

Writing the Alphabet

Trace and write the uppercase letter **W** and the lowercase letter **w**. Then trace and write the uppercase letter **X** and the lowercase letter **x**.

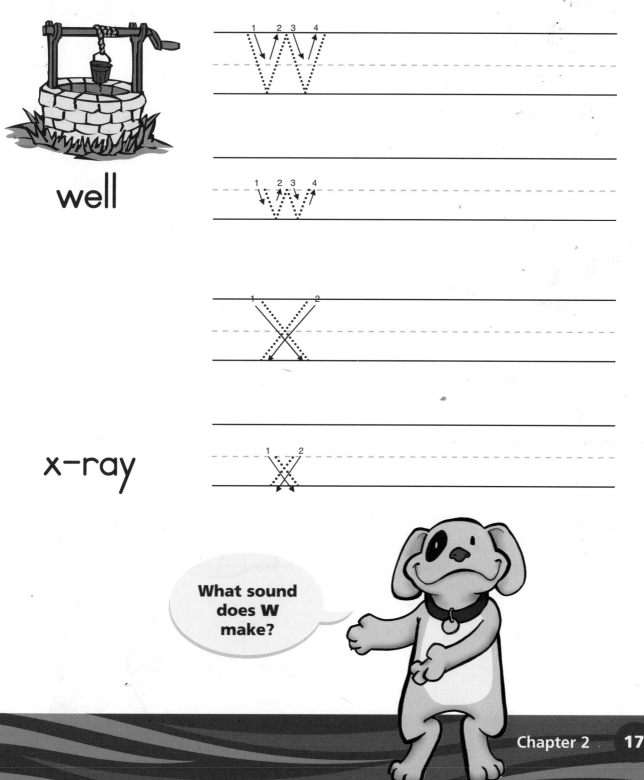

well

x-ray

What sound does **W** make?

Writing Missing Numbers

Write the missing numbers.

Let's go fishing!

Which Group Has More?

How many objects are in each group? Write the number in the blank. Circle the group that has more objects.

Count a group. Then write the number.

5

3

Good job!

Assessment

Chapter 2 Review

In this chapter, your child studied counting, beginning sounds, and how to write numbers and alphabet letters.

Your child learned how to:
- Write uppercase and lowercase letters.
- Phonetically recognize the letter K.
- Count objects in a group.
- Recognize number sequences.

To review what your child has learned, do the activities below. Go back through the pages of this chapter with your child if he or she is having difficulty in any of the following areas. You can also review and reinforce the skills of this section with the additional activities listed below.

1. Have your child write the numerals zero through nine in order.

2. Tell your child to write the beginning letter of his or her first name, and then list three things that begin with the same sound.

3. Ask your child to count and then write the number of items that are in each of the following groups:

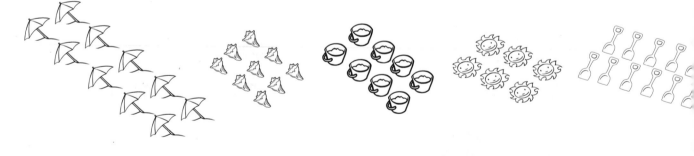

_____   _____   _____   _____   _____

Additional Activities
Below are some interactive ways you and your child can practice what you have worked on in this chapter. These activities will reinforce the skills your child studied on the previous pages.

1. Write uppercase and lowercase letters on a piece of paper. Cut them apart and have your child find each pair of letters.
2. Use 40 cards in a deck of cards. Shuffle them. Have your child separate them into groups according to suit. Count the number of cards in each group.
3. Choose a letter in the alphabet. Discuss the sound it makes. Have your child find items in your home that begin with that letter.

Chapter 3

Today's lesson will be lots of fun as we join Paige, Quincy, and Sam as they play in the surf!

While they explore, you will have a good time learning:
- Letters with lines
- Letters with both lines and curves
- Beginning sounds
- Objects in a group

Now let's see what's going on at the beach!

Writing the Alphabet

Trace and write the uppercase letter **Y** and the lowercase letter **y.** Then trace and write the uppercase letter **Z** and the lowercase letter **z.**

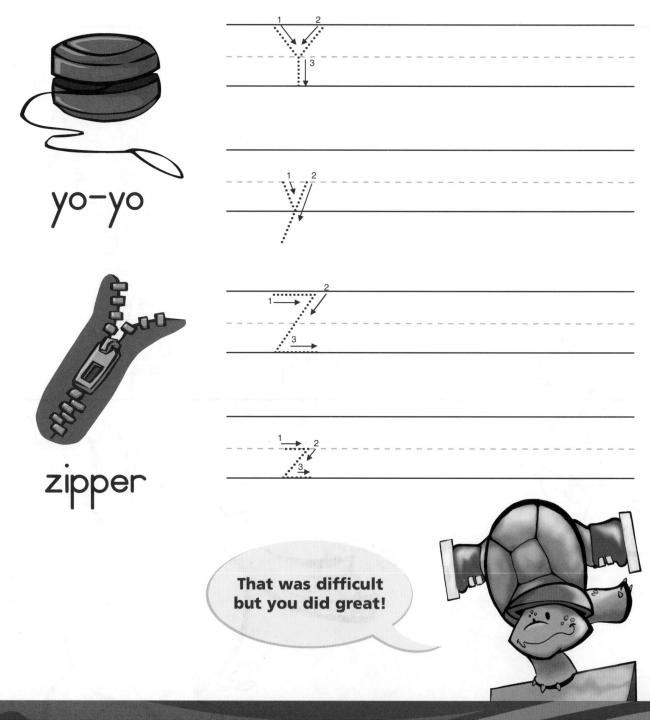

yo-yo

zipper

That was difficult but you did great!

Writing the Alphabet

Trace and then write the uppercase letter **A** and the lowercase letter **a**.

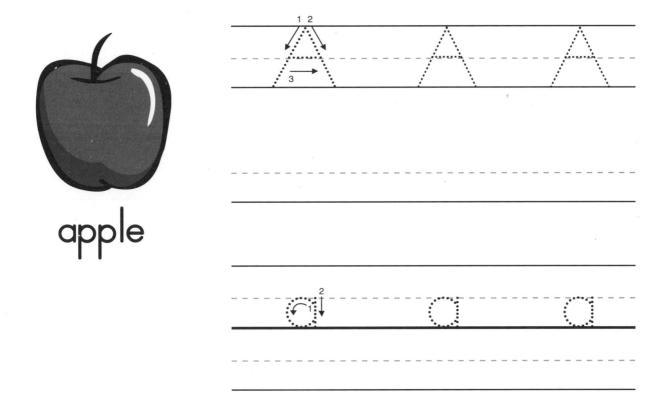

apple

Uppercase letters are bigger than lowercase letters!

Writing the Alphabet

Trace and then write the uppercase letter **B** and the lowercase letter **b**.

bee

Do you know any words that start with **B**?

Beginning Sounds: b

Marco and Sam are finding lots of exciting things on the island! Circle the pictures whose names begin with the same sound as **balloon.**

balloon

Can you think of other words that begin with the **b** sound?

Counting Objects in a Group

Count the objects and write the number.

Wow! You're doing great!

Assessment

Chapter 3 Review

Your child studied uppercase and lowercase letters, beginning sounds, and counting in this chapter. Because repetition is an effective method to reinforce learning, some exercises in this chapter were similar.

Your child learned how to:
- • Write uppercase and lowercase letters.
- • Recognize beginning letter sounds.
- • Count objects in a group.

To review what your child has learned, do the activities below. Go back throught the pages of this chapter if he or she is having difficulty in any of the following areas. You can also review and reinforce the skills in this section with the additional activities listed below.

1. Tell your child to draw a line to connect the lowercase letter with the corresponding uppercase letter.

b		Z
a		Y
z		B
y		A

2. Have your child put an X on the pictures that do not start with the letter B.

3. Ask your child to look at the numbers. On a separate piece of paper, have your child draw pictures to demonstrate the number written.

8   12   14   9   10

Additional Activities

Here are some simple and fun activities you can do with your child to practice what you have worked on in this chapter. These activities will reinforce the skills your child studied on the previous pages.

1. Have your child write a letter and then find two of his/her toys that begin with that letter.
2. Cut long pieces of yarn. Have your child make letters and numbers with the yarn.
3. Pour a small amount of cereal into a bowl. Have your child count the number of pieces.

Chapter 4

Today's lesson will be lots of fun as we join Quincy and Rosa while they trek through the deep jungle!

While they explore, you will have a good time learning:
- Letters with lines and curves
- Beginning sounds
- Objects in groups

Now let's see what's going on in the jungle!

Writing the Alphabet

Trace and then write the uppercase
letter **D** and the lowercase letter **d**.

dog

Beginning Sounds: d

Help Sam get to the date tree! Draw a line connecting the pictures whose names begin with the same sound as **dog.**

Writing the Alphabet

Trace and then write the uppercase letter **E** and the lowercase letter **e**.

elephant

I see an elephant!

Counting Objects in a Group

Count how many objects are in each group. Color the objects in each group to match the color of the numbers.

14　9　17

Gathering Information

How many red 👕s do you see? ___3___

How many blue 🧢s do you see? _____

How many black 🧦s do you see? _____

How many yellow 📒s do you see? _____

How many purple ✏s do you see? _____

Good work!

Assessment

Chapter 4 Review

In this chapter, your child learned lessons in counting, beginning sounds, alphabet letters, and gathering information.

Your child learned how to:
- Write uppercase and lowercase letters.
- Recognize beginning letter sound D.
- Count objects in a group.
- Comprehend information gathering.

To review what your child has learned, do the activities below. Go back through the pages of this chapter with your child if he or she is having difficulty in any of the following areas. You can also review and reinforce the skills of this section with the additional activities listed below.

1. Ask your child to list three things that begin with the same sound as dog.

2. Have your child name the three items on page 30 of this chapter that do not start with the letter D.

3. Tell your child to count the total number of hats. _____

   Then, have him or her count the total number of books. _____

Additional Activities

Below are some interactive ways you and your child can practice what you have worked on in this chapter. These activities will reinforce the skills your child studied on the previous pages.

1. Gather ten of your child's toys. Make a path on the floor using the toys. Tell your child which toy to walk to by giving him or her the beginning letter of the toy you are thinking of.
2. Gather a handful of different coins. Separate the coins by type of coin. Count the number of coins in each group.
3. Go to your child's sock drawer. Ask your child to count the number of a certain color or type of sock.

Chapter 5

Today's lesson will be lots of fun as we join Rosa, Bogart, and Sam visiting their friends in the zoo!

While they explore, you will have a good time learning:
• Letters with lines and curves
• Number order

Now let's see what's going on at the zoo!

Writing the Alphabet

Trace and then write the uppercase letter **F** and the lowercase letter **f.**

frog

What kind of animal lives in a pond?

Beginning Sounds: f

Sam can see many interesting things on this island! Circle the things he found that begin with the same sound as **fish**.

Writing the Alphabet

Trace and then write the uppercase letter **G** and the lowercase letter **g**.

grass

The word **grass** starts with the letter **G**.

What Number Comes After?

Great job!

Let's climb the ladder.

Read the number on each ladder. Write the number that comes **after** it.

What number comes after 6?

7

What number comes after 11?

_____

What number comes after 3?

_____

What number comes after 8?

_____

What number comes after 19?

_____

What number comes after 13?

_____

You're doing well!

What Number Is in the Middle?

Write the number that is in the **middle** of the numbers shown on the blocks.

Assessment

Chapter 5 Review

In this chapter, your child studied order, beginning sounds, and basic number recognition, while also learning how to write alphabet letters.

Your child studied:
- Uppercase and lowercase letters.
- The beginning sound of letter F.
- Number order.

To review what your child has learned, do the activities below. Go back through the pages of this chapter if he or she is having difficulty in any of the following areas. You can also review and reinforce the skills in this section with the additional activities listed below.

1. Ask your child to list the two items on page 37 of this chapter that do not begin with the letter F. With what letters do the other two items begin?

   _____ _____

2. Have your child answer the questions about each number.

   What number comes after 10? _____

   What number comes in the middle of 13 and 15? _____

   What number comes in the middle of your first answer and the number 13? _____

3. Fill in the blanks with the correct number.

   10, _____, 12, 13, _____, _____, 16, _____, 18, _____, 20

Additional Activities
Here are some simple and fun activities you can do with your child to practice what you have worked on in this chapter. These activities will reinforce the skills your child studied on the previous pages.

1. Have your child practice writing uppercase and lowercase letters in shaving cream that has been spread on the floor of a bathtub or shower.
2. Roll a pair of dice. Have your child tell what number or numbers are in the middle of the numbers on each die. (If you roll a 3 and a 6, the answer is 4 and 5.)
3. Using a calculator, show your child a number. Have your child show you the number that comes next by typing it into the calculator.

Chapter 6

Today's lesson will be lots of fun as we join Rosa while she dances in the desert!

While she dances, you will have a good time learning:
- Letters with lines and curves
- Beginning sounds
- Number order

Now let's see what's going on in the desert!

Writing the Alphabet

Trace and then write the uppercase letter **H** and the lowercase letter **h**.

hat

Marco left his **hat** in the garden.

Beginning Sounds: h

Say the name of each picture. If the picture's name begins with the same sound as **horse,** circle **yes.** If not, circle **no.**

yes   no

horse

yes   no

yes   no

yes   no

yes   no

yes   no

yes   no

Hooray for you!

Writing the Alphabet

Trace and then write the uppercase letter **J** and the lowercase letter **j**.

jam

Beginning Sounds: j

Draw lines from the **j** to the pictures that begin with the letter **j**.

Great job!

What Numbers Come Before and After?

Circle the child who is counting his or her numbers in numerical order.

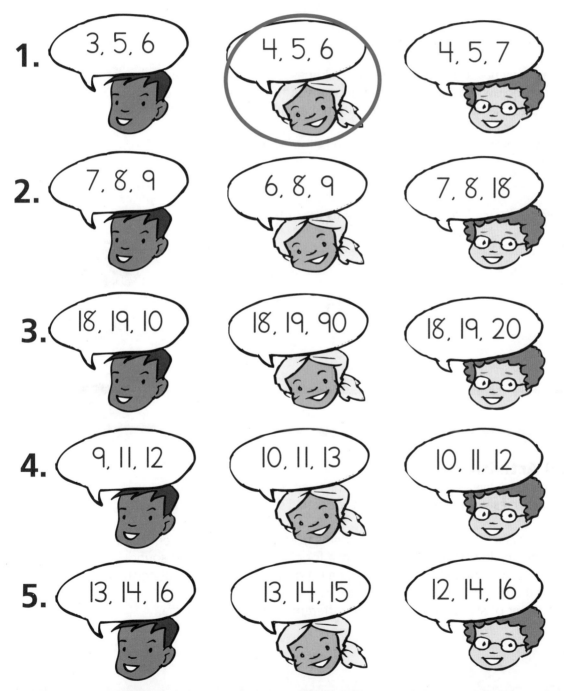

1. 3, 5, 6   4, 5, 6   4, 5, 7

2. 7, 8, 9   6, 8, 9   7, 8, 18

3. 18, 19, 10   18, 19, 90   18, 19, 20

4. 9, 11, 12   10, 11, 13   10, 11, 12

5. 13, 14, 16   13, 14, 15   12, 14, 16

Assessment

Chapter 6 Review

In this chapter, your child studied beginning sounds, number order, and how to write alphabet letters.

Your child studied:
- Uppercase and lowercase letters.
- The beginning sounds of letters H and J.
- The correct number order.

Do the following activities to review what your child has learned. If your child is having difficulty in any of the areas below, go back through the pages of this chapter with your child. You can also review and reinforce the skills in this section with the additional activities listed below.

1. Ask your child to write the numbers that come before and after each number given.

    ____ 9 _____   _____ 14 ____   ____ 8 _____   _____ 18 _____

2. Tell your child to draw a line from the picture to the letter with which it begins.

Additional Activities
Below are some interactive ways you and your child can review what you have worked on in this chapter. These activities will reinforce the skills your child studied on the previous pages.

1. Choose two letters in the alphabet. Gather items from your home that begin with each letter. Have your child sort the items into a pile for each beginning letter sound.
2. Use the first letter in your child's name. Write a list of all of the things that he/she can see in your home that begin with the same letter.
3. Count the number of steps it takes to get to different rooms in your home.

Chapter 7

Today's lesson will be lots of fun as we join Sam flying through deep space in a flying saucer!

While he explores, you will have a good time learning:
- Letters with lines and curves
- Beginning sounds
- Ending sounds
- Number order

Now let's see what's going on in outer space!

Writing the Alphabet

Trace and write the uppercase letter **M** and the lowercase letter **m**. Then trace and write the uppercase letter **N** and lowercase letter **n**.

mouse

nut

Nice work!

Beginning Sounds: m

Let's do some sorting! Find the pictures whose names begin with the same sound as **monkey.** Draw lines from those pictures to the box.

monkey

Can you think of more words that begin with **m?**

Beginning Sounds: n

Bogart takes a net with him as he explores. Circle the pictures whose names begin with the same sound as **net.**

Do you hear the **n** sound at the beginning of the word net?

Same Ending Sounds

Match the words that have the same ending sound.

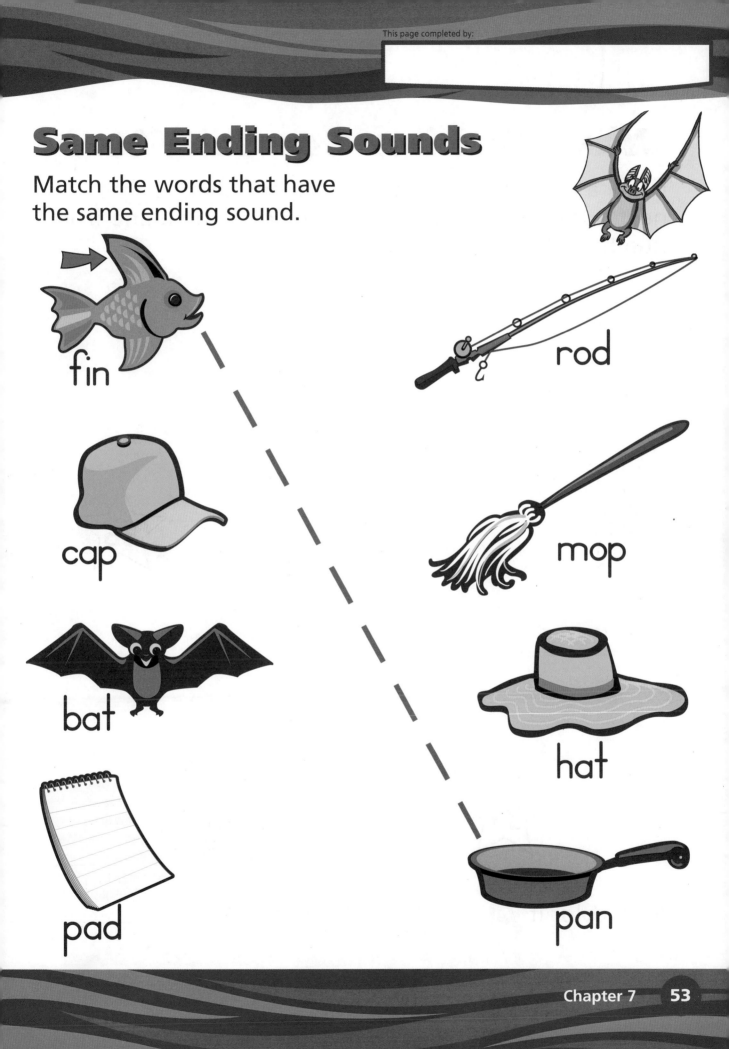

fin

rod

cap

mop

bat

hat

pad

pan

What Number Comes After?

Draw a line from each star to the one that has the next number. Finish the picture by drawing a line from number 37 to number 33.

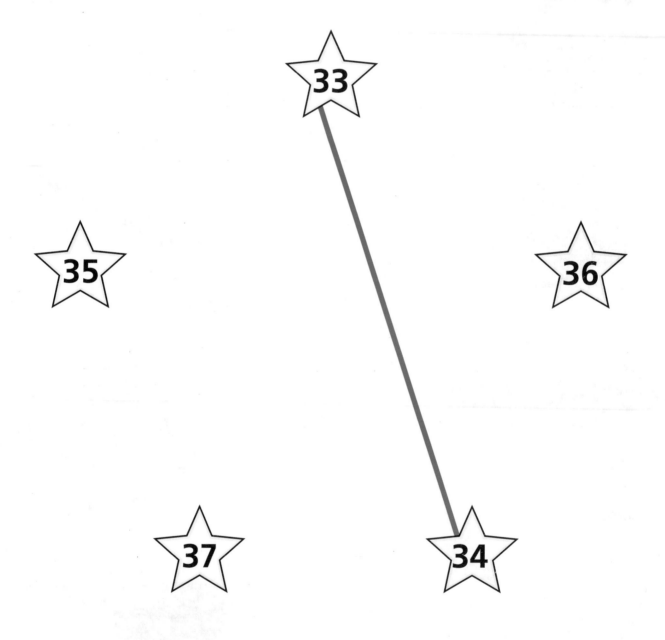

Now color it yellow! What did you make? _____

Assessment

Chapter 7 Review

In this chapter, your child studied uppercase and lowercase letters, beginning and ending sounds, and number order.

Your child studied:
- Uppercase and lowercase letters.
- Phonetic recognition for the letters M and N.
- Recognition of the same ending sounds.
- Number order.

The following activities will allow your child to review the lessons studied in this chapter. If your child is having difficulty in any of the areas below, review the pages of this chapter with your child. You can also review and reinforce the skills covered in this chapter with the additional activities at the bottom of this page.

1. Have your child look at the pictures and fill in the ending sound of each word.

pi_　　　　ma_　　　　ba_　　　　ca_　　　　ma_

2. Next to each number, write the number that comes next.

23 ___　　28____　　31_____　　37 _____　　39_____

Additional Activities

Here are some simple and fun things you can do with your child to practice what you have worked on in this chapter. To help reinforce what was learned in this chapter, try these activities.

1. Make a list of the ages of your family members. Have your child tell you how old each person will be on his/her next birthday.
2. Choose any ten numbers in order. Create a dot-to-dot picture of your own using the numbers you chose as the dots. Have your child guess what the picture will be. Have your child connect the dots to see if his or her guess was correct.
3. Have your child write the ending sounds of the names of favorite story characters.

Chapter 8

Today's lesson will be lots of fun as we join Marco diving down to the ocean floor!

While he explores, you will have a good time learning:
- Letters with lines and curves
- Beginning sounds
- Counting numbers
- Illustrating numbers

Now let's see what's happening on the ocean floor!

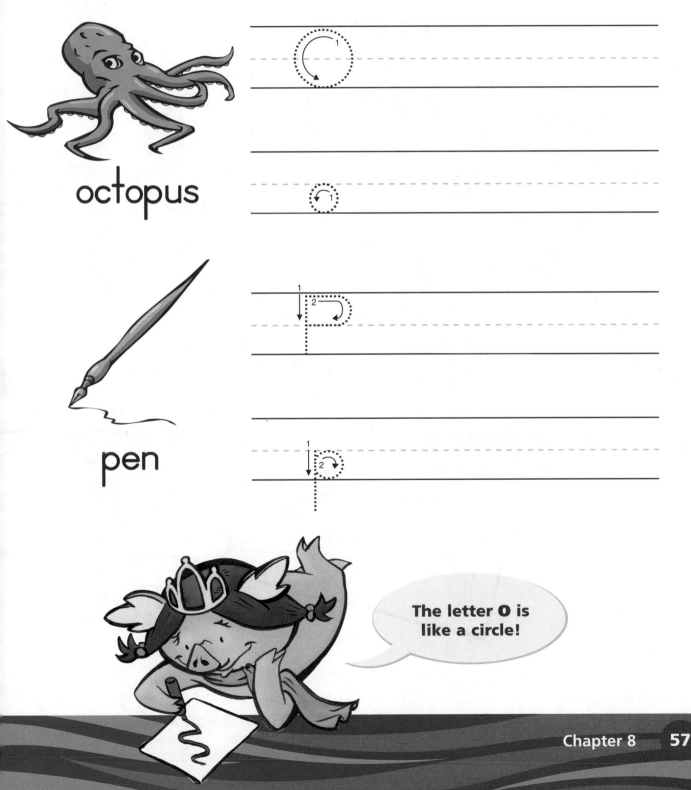

Writing the Alphabet

Trace and write the uppercase letter **O** and the lowercase letter **o**. Then trace and write the uppercase letter **P** and the lowercase letter **p**.

octopus

pen

The letter **O** is like a circle!

Beginning Sounds: p

Bogart is having a picnic! He will only eat foods that begin with the **p** sound. Cross out the foods that do <u>not</u> begin with the same sound as **pot.**

Writing Numbers

Trace each number.

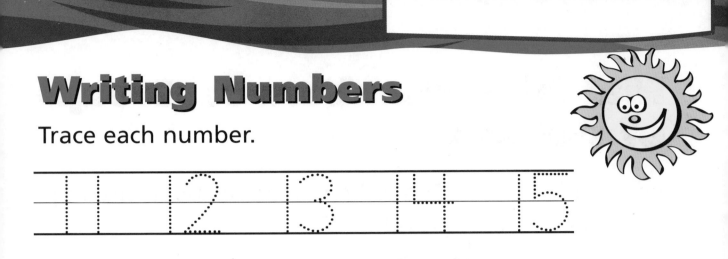

11 12 13 14 15

How many objects do you count? Draw a line from the number to the objects that have that number.

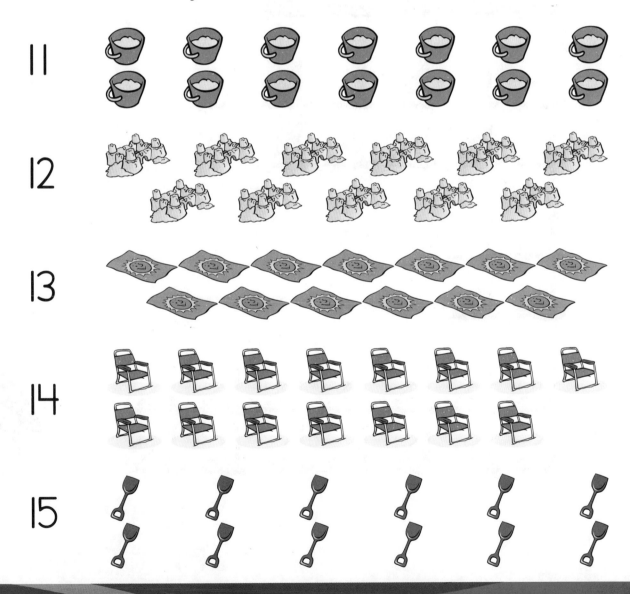

11

12

13

14

15

Matching Numbers to Groups of Objects

Read each number. Draw the number of boats missing from the group to match the number.

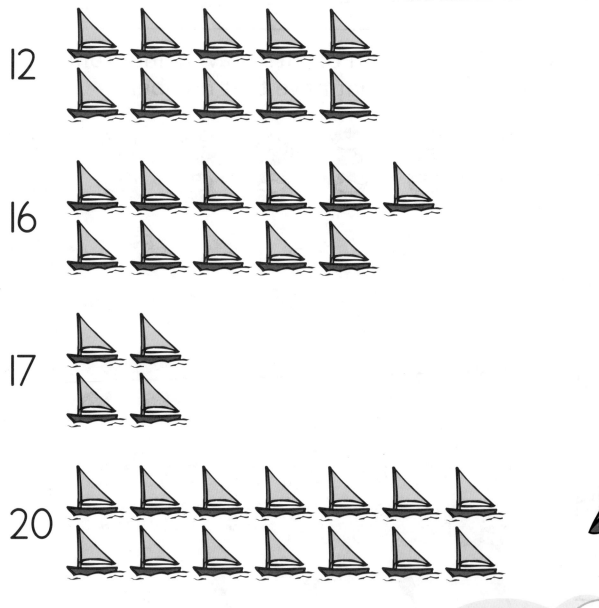

12

16

17

20

Nice work!

Drawing Objects in a Group

Draw the objects to match the number.

11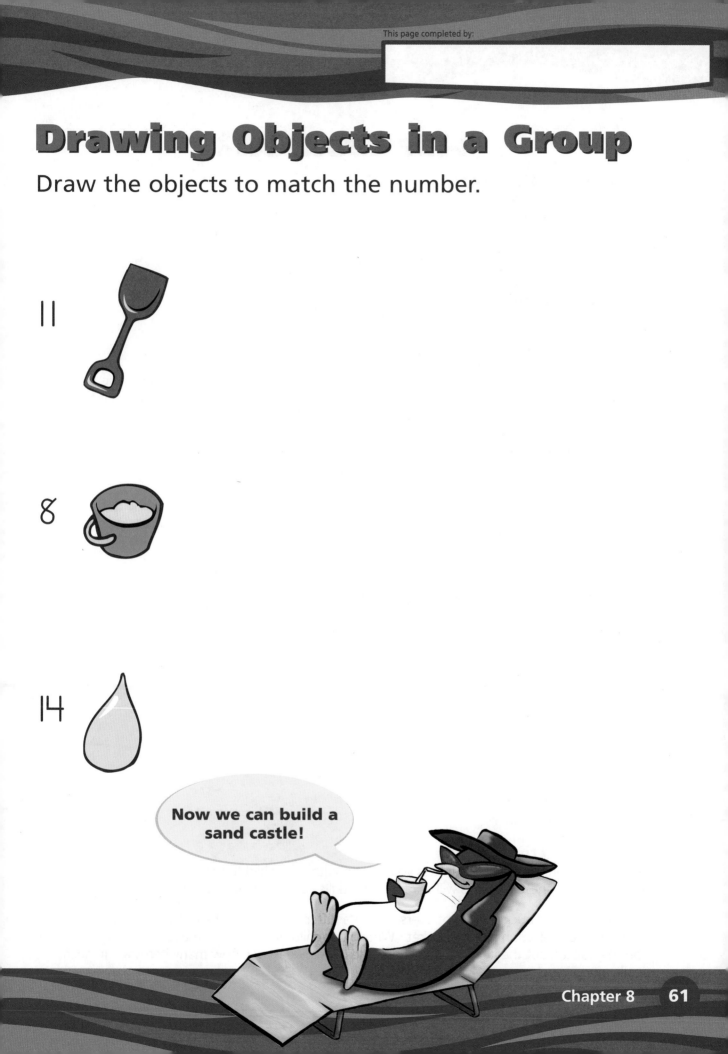

8

14

Now we can build a
sand castle!

Assessment

Chapter 8 Review

In this chapter, your child studied beginning sounds and numbers, counting, and how to write the alphabet. Because repetition is an effective method to reinforce learning, some exercises in this chapter were similar.

Your child learned how to:
- Write uppercase and lowercase letters.
- Recognize the beginning sound of letter P.
- Count objects in a group.
- Match numbers to groups of objects.

To review what your child has learned, do the three activities below. Go back through the pages of this chapter if your child is having difficulty in any of the following areas. You can also review and reinforce the skills in this section with the additional activities listed below.

1. Ask your child to list three things at school that begin with the P sound.

_____   _____   _____

2. Have your child count the numbers in each group and then write the number of items in each group on the lines below.

_____   _____   _____   _____   _____

3. On a separate sheet of paper, help your child:
   Draw 12 favorite foods.
   Draw 14 favorite things about summer.
   Draw 11 favorite animals.

Additional Activities

Here are some simple and fun activities you can do with your child to practice what you have worked on in Chapter 8. These activities will reinforce the skills your child learned on the previous pages.

1. Gather a few old buckets or containers. Write a different letter on the outside of each bucket. Start a letter collection in each bucket. When your child finds an item that begins with the letter on the bucket, put the item inside. At the end of the week, see how many items are in each collection.

Chapter 9

Today's lesson will be lots of fun as we join Rosa and Quincy as they look for Marco the penguin on the ocean shore!

While they investigate, you will have a good time learning:
- Letters with lines and curves
- Beginning sounds
- Counting
- Number identification and number words

Writing the Alphabet

Trace and write the uppercase letter **Q** and the lowercase letter **q.** Then trace and write the uppercase letter **R** and the lowercase letter **r.**

queen

ring

An uppercase **Q** is like a circle with a little line through it!

Beginning Sounds: r

Rosa notices a lot of things that begin with the **r** sound on her walk along the beach. Find six of these things in this picture and circle them.

rose

Drawing Pictures to Show Data

There are 6 girls and 5 boys in Quincy's class. Draw a picture to show the girls and boys in his class.

What a good-looking group of kids!

Matching Groups, Words, and Numbers

Draw a line from the number word to it's matching numeral. Next draw a line from the numeral to the picture that has the same number of balls as the numeral. Finish by coloring the balls.

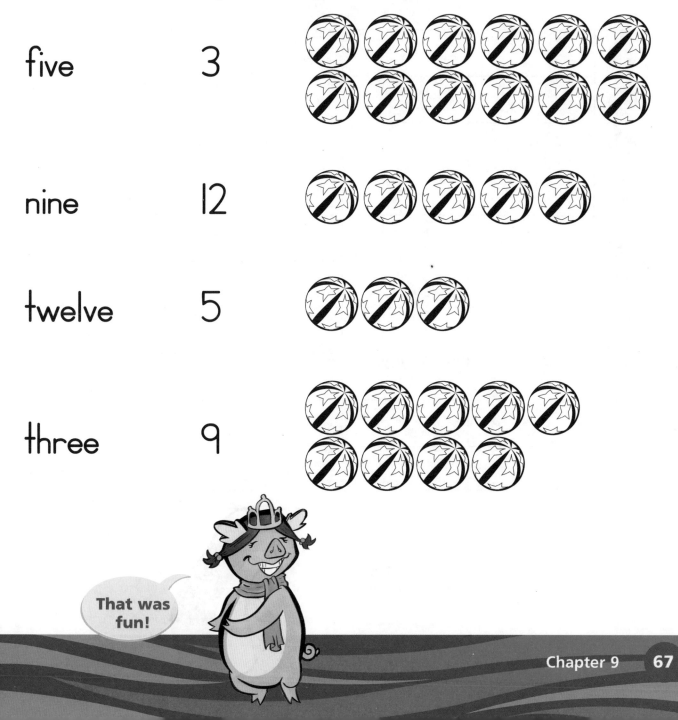

five   3

nine   12

twelve   5

three   9

That was fun!

Modeling Numbers from 1 to 10

Find your way from top to bottom. Starting at row 1, find the cell that has the same number of stars as the row number, drawing a line as you go along. Continue down until you end in row 10.

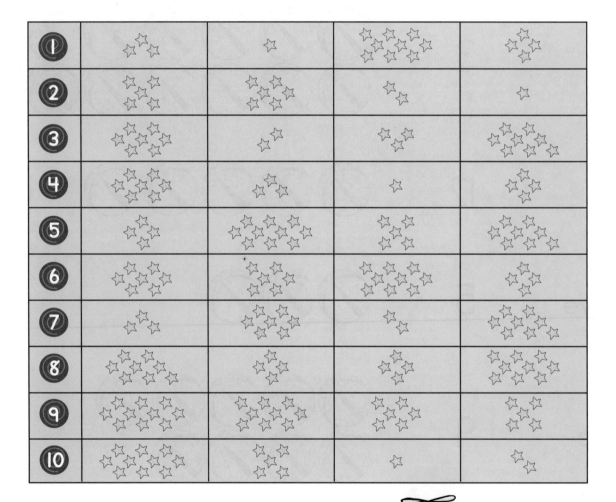

Way to go!

Assessment

Chapter 9 Review

In Chapter 9, your child studied uppercase and lowercase letters, phonetics, and counting.

Your child learned how to:
- Identifify letters.
- Phonetically recognize the letter R.
- Count objects in a group.
- Model numbers.

To review what your child has learned, do the activities below. Go back through the pages of this chapter if your child is having difficulty in any of the following areas. You can also review and reinforce the skills in this section with the additional activities listed below.

1. Ask your child to read the number word and draw the correct number of circles next to the word.

Three _____   Five _____   Nine _____

2. Have your child find the cell that has the same number of stars as the row number. Tell her or him to put an X on that cell.

3. Have your child write two things that can be seen on the way to school that begin with the R sound.

_____   _____

Additional Activities
Here are some simple and fun things you can do with your child to practice what you have worked on in this chapter.

1. On one half of a 3x5 card, write a number word and the number. On the other half, have your child draw the correct number of objects. Do this on 5 or 6 cards. Cut the cards apart. Mix them up and have your child put them back together.
2. Choose a letter in the alphabet. While reading a story with your child, look for pictures that begin with the letter sound you have chosen.

Chapter 10

Today's lesson will be lots of fun as we join Paige and Quincy as they visit the zoo!

While they explore, you will have a good time learning:
- Letters with lines and curves
- Beginning sounds
- Number words
- The concept of less than

Now let's see what's happening at the zoo!

ZOO

Writing the Alphabet

Trace and write the uppercase letter **S** and the lowercase letter **s**. Then trace and write the uppercase letter **T** and the lowercase letter **t**.

snake

turtle

What words do you know that start with T?

Beginning Sounds: s

Draw lines to connect the pictures that begin with the same sound as **seal.** Try to make a square!

Square begins with the s sound!

Beginning Sounds: t

Color the pictures that begin with the same sound as **turtle**.

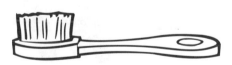

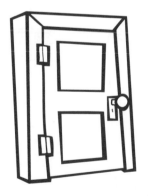

Can you say this?
Ten turtles trick two tired tigers!

Which Group Has Fewer?

How many objects are in each group? Count the objects and write the number in the blank. Circle the group that has fewer objects.

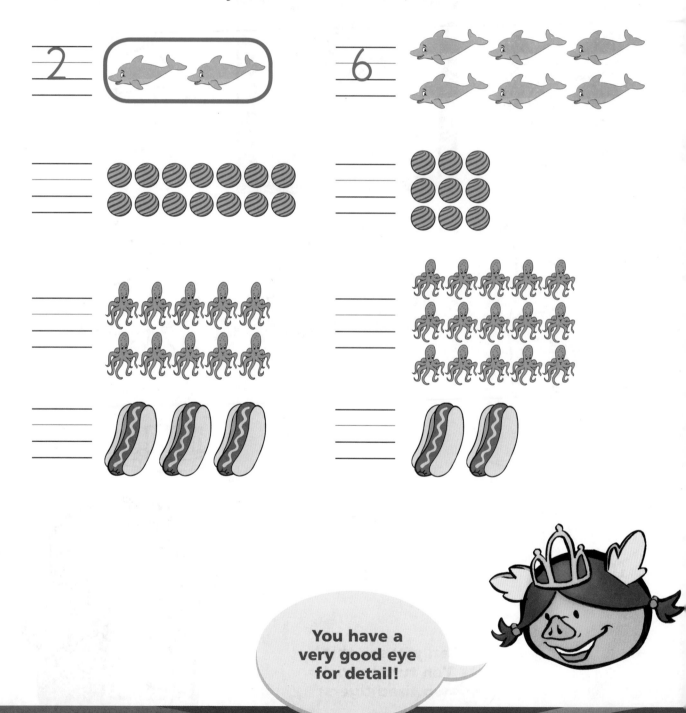

You have a very good eye for detail!

Assessment

Chapter 10 Review

In this chapter, your child studied phonetics, counting, word numbers, and learned how to write uppercase and lowercase letters.

Your child learned how to:
- Identify letters.
- Phonetically recognize the letters S and T.
- Count objects in a group.
- Match words and numbers.

Do the following activities to review what your child has learned. If your child is having difficulty in any of the areas below, go back through the pages of this chapter with your child. With the additional activities listed below, you can also review and reinforce the skills covered in this chapter.

1. Ask your child to circle the pictures that begin with a T and draw an X on the pictures that begin with S.

2. Have your child think of a different item for each number and draw the correct number of items on a separate sheet of paper.

6   10   7   9

3. For each group, have your child draw the pictures to show one less item. Use a separate sheet of paper.

Additional Activities

Here are some interactive ways you and your child can practice what you have worked on in this chapter. These activities will reinforce the skills your child studied on the previous pages.

1. Have your child try to form uppercase and lowercase letters using his/her body. Do this activity with family and friends.
2. Choose a letter in the alphabet. Go to the library with your child and find books with topics that begin with the letter you chose.
3. Gather groups of items in your child's room. Label them with the correct number and number word.

Chapter 11

Today's lesson will be lots of fun as we join Marco and Rosa as they hike through the forest!

While they explore, you will have a good time learning about:

- Letters with lines and curves
- ABC letter order
- Numbers and number words
- Skip counting by tens
- Number sets

Writing the Alphabet

Trace and write the uppercase letter **U** and the lowercase letter **u.** Then trace and write the uppercase letter **V** and the lowercase letter **v.**

umbrella

vine

You have written nearly all the letters of the alphabet. Great!

Letters in ABC Order

Sam is looking at an alphabet book, but some of the letters are out of order. Circle the letters that are not in ABC order.

A   B   L   C

D   M   E   F

Matching Words to Numbers

Match each word to its number. Draw a line from the sand castle to the pail with the same number.

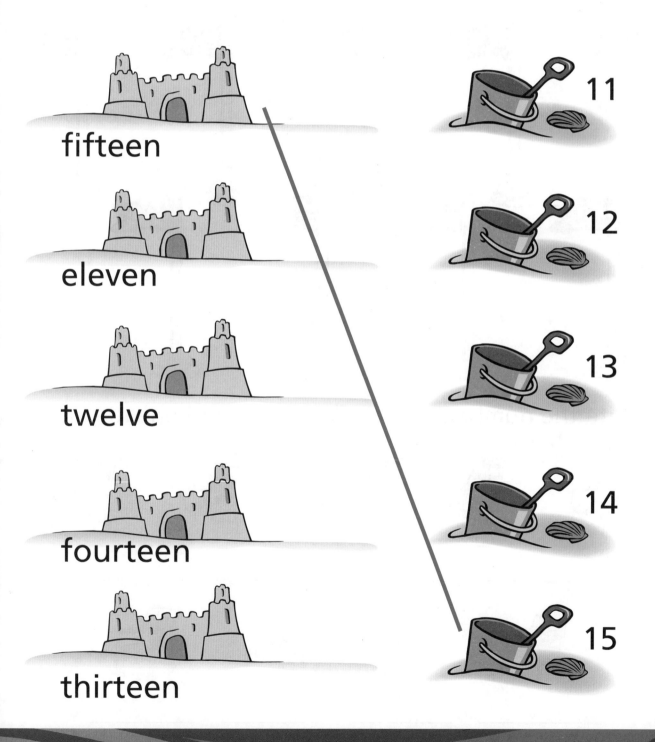

fifteen

eleven

twelve

fourteen

thirteen

11

12

13

14

15

Counting by 10's

Quincy works at the beach. Every morning, he places a flag behind each lifeguard's chair.

Write the numbers on the flags in order beneath the beach chairs.

20 _____ _____ _____ _____

_____ _____ _____ _____

Chapter 12

Today's lesson will be lots of fun as we join Quincy and Rosa as they fly high in the sky!

While they explore, you will have a good time learning about:
• ABC letter order
• Number lines

Now let's see what's happening up in the clouds!

Letters in ABC Order

Fill in the blank line with the letter that comes next.

S T ___ V

W ___ Y ___

You've reached the end of the alphabet!

Letters in ABC Order

Fill in the missing letters.

A ___ C D

I J K ___

U ___ W X

M N ___ P

E ___ G H

Sing your favorite alphabet song for help!

Letters in ABC Order

Fill in the missing letters.

Great job!

Making a Number Line

Write the number from the number line that goes with each animal on the spaces below.

3 ___ ___ ___ ___ ___

The numbers on a number line are in order from the lowest number to the highest number.

Using a Number Line

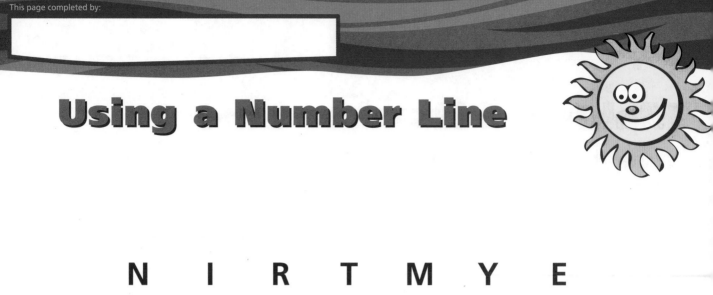

```
N   I   R   T   M   Y   E
+---+---+---+---+---+---+---
1   2   3   4   5   6   7
```

Use the number line to find Sam's missing item.
Write the letter above the number it matches on
the number line.

<u> M </u>   <u>   </u>   <u>   </u>   <u>   </u>   <u>   </u>   <u>   </u>

  5   2   4   4   7   1

The numbers on the number line are in order from smallest to largest.

Assessment

Chapter 12 Review

Your child studied alphabetical order and numerical order in this chapter.

Your child learned:
- Alphabetization.
- Comprehension and use of number lines.

To review what your child has learned, do the activities below. If your child is having difficulty in any of the areas below, go back and review the pages with him or her. You can also review and reinforce the skills in this section with the additional activities listed below.

1. Ask your child to fill in the missing letters.

A___ C D ____ F G H ____ J ____ ____ M ____

2. Have your child fill in the missing numbers on the number line:

3. Tell your child to use the number line to fill in the missing letters:

Before I go to bed, I should brush my:

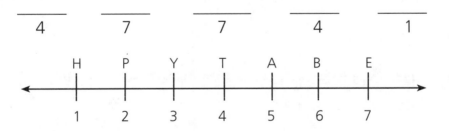

Additional Activities

Below are some interactive ways you and your child can review what you have worked on in this chapter. These activities will reinforce the skills your child studied on the previous pages.

1. Use magnetic letters and have your child put them in alphabetical order. Take any 4 or 5 letters, mix them up, and then have your child put them back in order.
2. Make a number line with corresponding letters. Have your child figure out the "secret word" using the number line.
3. On a car trip with your child, say a group of letters out loud and pause. See if your child can tell you what comes next.

Chapter 13

Today's lesson will be lots of fun as we join Quincy and Rosa as they relax in their playhouse!

While they explore, you will have a good time learning about:
- ABC letter order
- Picture Graphs
- Bar Graphs

Now let's see what's happening at the playhouse!

Letters in ABC Order

Connect the letters in ABC order to
make a picture. Start at the letter **k**.

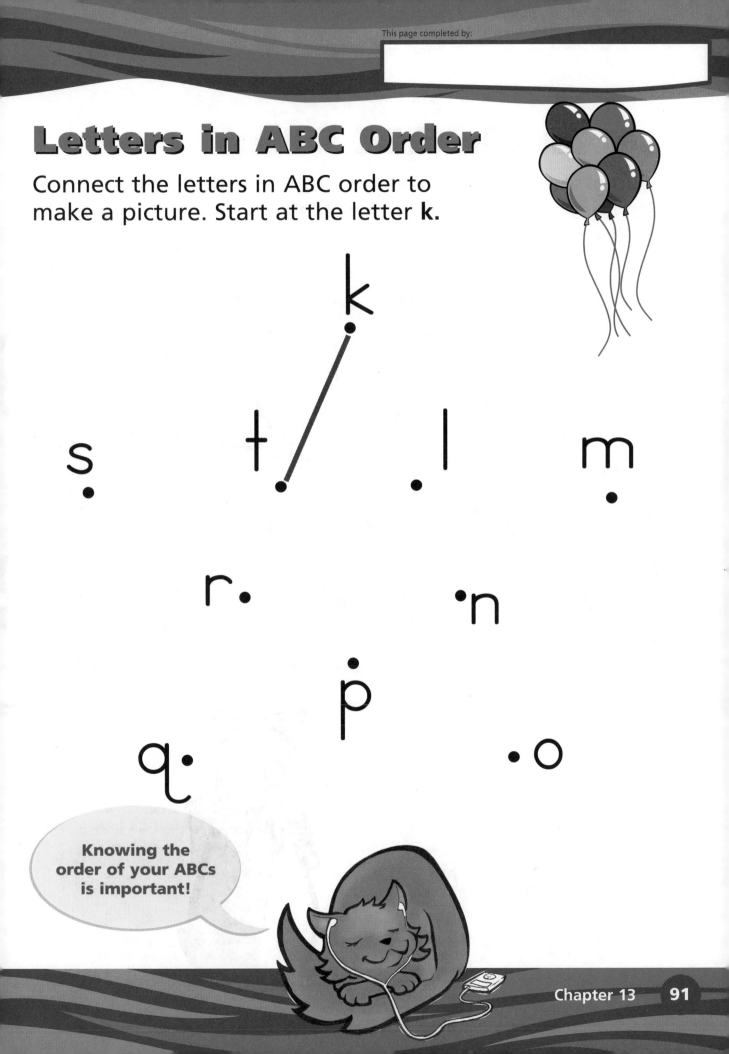

k

t   l   m

s

r   n

p

q   o

**Knowing the
order of your ABCs
is important!**

Letters in ABC Order

Marco sees letters in the clouds, but some letters are missing. Write the missing letters in ABC order on the clouds.

The ABCs are just everywhere!

Grouping

Draw a  for each letter in each child's name.

Reading a Vertical Bar Graph

Look at this bar graph of Mrs. Truman's class.

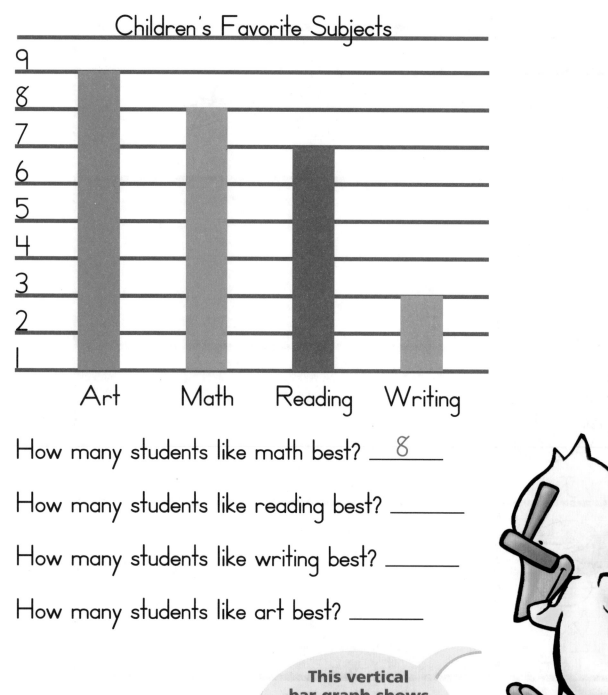

Children's Favorite Subjects

How many students like math best? ___8___

How many students like reading best? _____

How many students like writing best? _____

How many students like art best? _____

> This vertical bar graph shows information using bars that go from bottom to top.

Assessment

Chapter 13 Review

In this chapter, your child studied how to read and create graphs as well as alphabetical order.

Your child learned:
- Alphabetization.
- Comprehension of information presented in graphs.

To review what your child has learned, do the two activities below. Go back through the pages of this chapter if your child is having difficulty in any of the following areas. You can also review and reinforce the skills in this section with the additional activities listed below.

1. Ask your child to fill in the missing letters in ABC order.

L M N _____ P _____ R S T _____ V

2. Have your child survey family and friends about the pets they have in their homes, and then fill in this graph with the information.

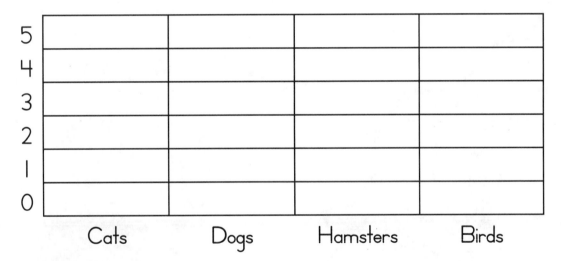

Additional Activities

Here are some simple and fun activities you can do with your child to practice what you have worked on in Chapter 13. These activities will reinforce the skills your child learned on the previous pages.

1. Write each letter of the alphabet on an index card. Mix them up and have your child put them in order from A to Z.
2. Get a piece of graph paper. Have your child think of 3 or 4 different sports or foods, and then ask as many people as possible which one is their favorite. Record it on the graph paper in the form of a vertical bar graph.

Chapter 14

Today's lesson will be lots of fun as we join Rosa and Bogart as they visit the zoo!

While they explore, you will have a good time learning about:
- ABC letter order
- Beginning sounds in words
- Recognizing same and different
- Counting

Now let's see what's happening at the zoo!

Words in ABC Order

Write the missing letters in ABC order.

1. _____ ion

2. _____ ice

3. _____ est

4. _____ wl

5. _____ ig

You're good at putting words in ABC order!

Picturing Things

Look carefully at the picture of a farm. Now look at the farm picture on the next page.

Circle the differences between the two farms.

Assessment

Chapter 14 Review

In Chapter 14, your child studied alphabetical order and object recognition.

Your child learned:
- Alphabetization.
- Object identification.
- Identification of differences between groups of objects.

To review what your child has learned, do the activities below. Go back through the pages of this chapter with your child if he or she is having difficulty in any of the following areas. You can also review and reinforce the skills of this section with the additional activities listed below.

1. Have your child fill in the missing letters in each group:

Q _____ S T

B C _____ E F_____

_____ K L M _____ O

2. Ask your child to write the missing letters in ABC order:

_____ ar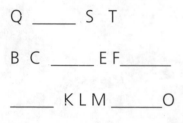

_____ ite

_____ ion

_____ice

Additional Activities

Here are some simple and fun things you can do with your child to practice what you have worked on in this chapter. To help reinforce what was learned in this chapter, try these activities

1. Have your child look carefully around the kitchen. Tell them to close their eyes or leave the room while you change something (turn the toaster around, open a cabinet, etc). Now have your child come back and see if he/she can tell you what is different.
2. Place a group of objects together on a table or tray. Include an object that obviously does not belong. Ask your child to pick out the object that does not belong.

Chapter 15

Today's lesson will be lots of fun as we join Rosa and Marco as they help out on the farm.

While they practice driving a tractor, you will have a good time learning:
- Beginning sounds
- Visual discrimination
- Counting objects
- Plane figure shape identification

Same Beginning Sounds

Paige is writing in the sand. Circle the words that start with the same sound.

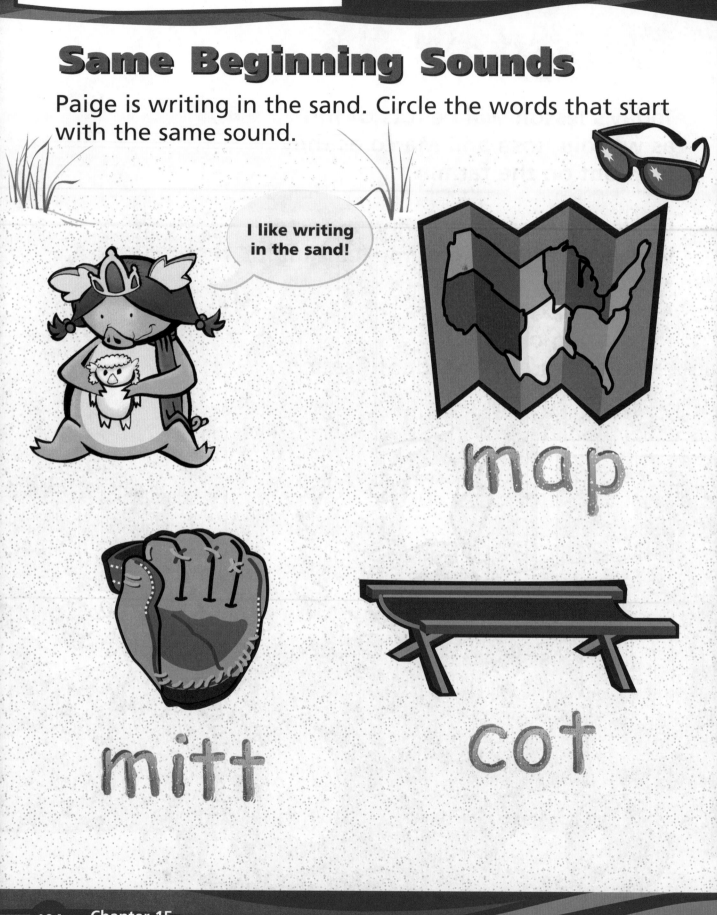

I like writing in the sand!

map

mitt

cot

Assessment

Chapter 15 Review

In this chapter, your child studied beginning sounds and identifying different shapes and objects.

Your child learned how to:
- Identify different shapes and objects.
- Beginning Sounds

Do the following activities to review what your child has learned. If your child is having difficulty in any of the areas below, go back through the pages of this chapter with him/her. You can also review and reinforce the skills in this section with the additional activities listed below.

1. Have your child circle the words with the same beginning sound:

milk   lion   mouse

2. Look at the words below. Circle the beginning letters that make the same sound:

ball   dog   bat

Additional Activities

Here are some simple and fun things you can do with your child to practice what you have worked on in this chapter. To help reinforce what was learned in this chapter, try these activities.

1. Have your child walk around the house and find as many things as possible that begin with the same sound.
2. Play a game with your child where you say two words and your child has to tell you whether or not they have the same beginning sound.
3. Find a container of pattern blocks. Have your child practice sorting the blocks by shape and color.

Chapter 16

Today's lesson will be lots of fun as we join Marco and Quincy while they explore a cave with unusual paintings!

While they explore, you will have a good time learning:
• Beginning sounds
• Sorting by attributes

Now let's see what's happening in the cave!

Same Beginning Sounds

Draw a line to connect the words with the same beginning sound.

bed

raccoon

key

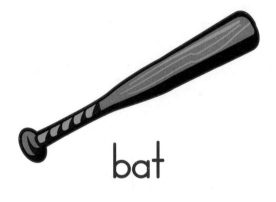

bat

ring

king

Same Beginning Sounds

Look at the picture below. Circle two things that have the same beginning sound.

sun

Good job!

book

Sam

Same Beginning Sounds

Say each word. Draw a line between the words that have the same beginning sound.

sun

pot

pin

nail

net

sock

Sorting Shapes by Size

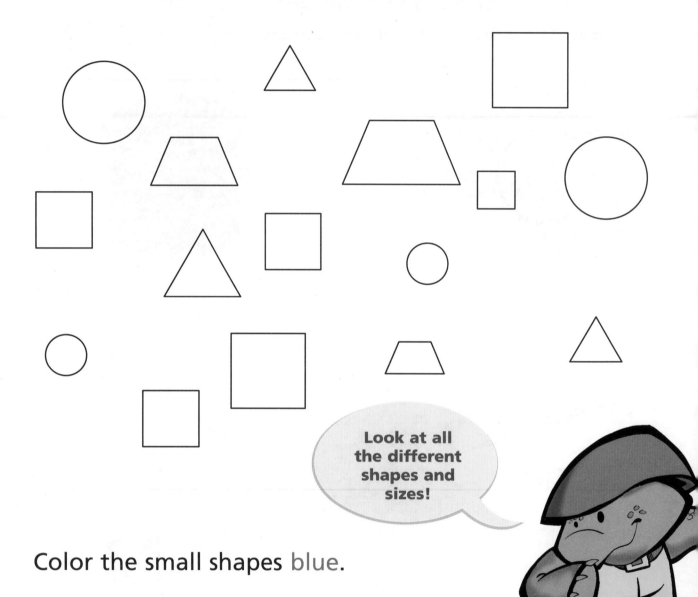

Look at all the different shapes and sizes!

Color the small shapes blue.

Color the medium shapes yellow.

Color the large shapes green.

Grouping by Size

Color the small objects blue.
Color the medium objects red.
Color the large objects green.

This is great!

Assessment

Chapter 16 Review

In Chapter 16, some activities were repeated to reinforce your child's learning. Your child studied initial sound recognition as well as shape and size identification.

Your child learned:
- Phonetic recognition of beginning sounds.
- Discernment of shapes by size.

To review what your child has learned, do the activities below. Go back through the pages of this chapter with your child if he or she is having difficulty in any of the following areas. You can also review and reinforce the skills of this section with the additional activities listed below.

1. Have your child draw a line to connect the words with the same beginning sounds.

kite   horn

pear   bed

hat   key

balloon   pineapple

2. Draw a circle around the small shapes and draw an X through the large ones.

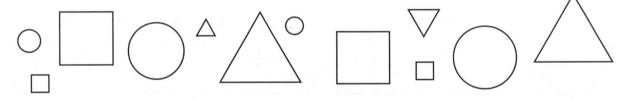

Additional Activities
Below are some interactive ways you and your child can review what you have worked on in this chapter. These activities will reinforce the skills your child studied on the previous pages.

1. Play the game, "I'm thinking of a word that begins like mitten," and your child should come up with a word with the same beginning sound.
2. Play "Memory" with beginning sounds. Turn cards over until you have two cards that have the same beginning sounds.
3. Collect a group of rocks or buttons. Sort them according to their size – small, medium, or large.

Chapter 17

Today's lesson will be lots of fun
as we join Quincy and Rosa rocketing
to the moon!

While they explore, you will
have a good time learning:
- Beginning sounds
- Single-digit addition
- Number operation signs

Now let's see what's happening
in outer space!

Same Beginning Sounds

Sam has lost his way to his beach blanket! Help him find his way back. Follow the words that have the same beginning sound.

sun
bird
pan
six
sad
cat
sock

Different Beginning Sounds

Circle the picture with the name that starts with a different sound than the others.

pot

sun

pen

pig

Say the words.
Are any of the sounds
you hear the same?

Adding Numbers 1 through 3

Help Paige collect apples. **Add** the apples to find their total number. Complete the number sentence.

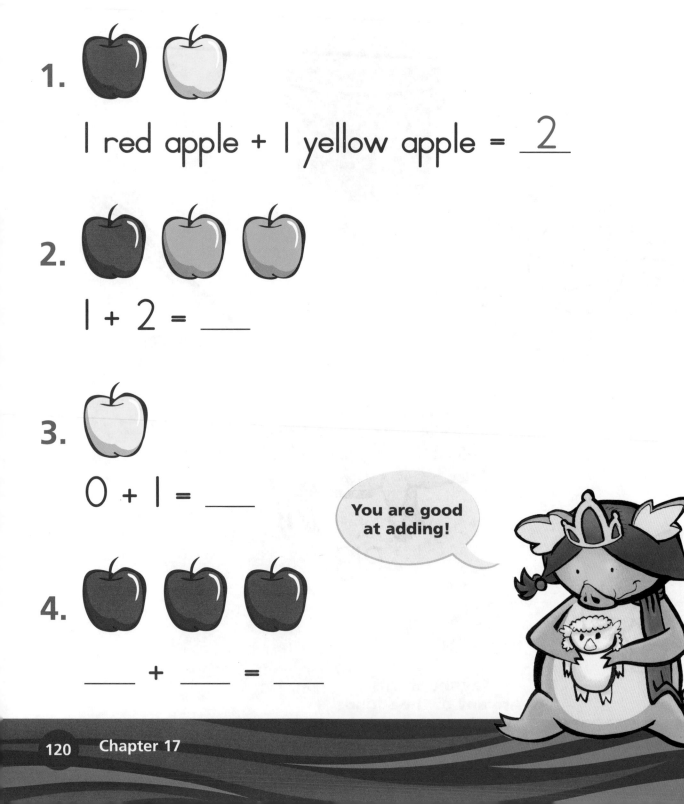

1. I red apple + I yellow apple = _2_

2. 1 + 2 = ___

3. 0 + 1 = ___

You are good at adding!

4. ___ + ___ = ___

Matching + and - Signs

Draw a line from each word to all of its symbols.
Then color each star to match its planet.

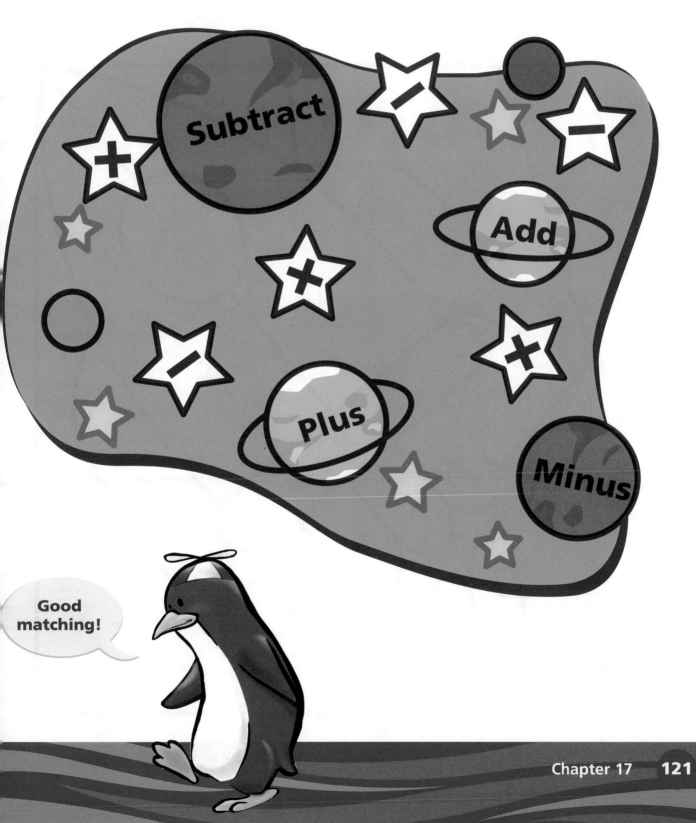

Good matching!

Matching Words

Color the sections red that have **plus** signs.
Color the sections blue that have **minus** signs.

Assessment

Chapter 17 Review

In Chapter 17, your child studied how to identify addition and subtraction signs, beginning sounds, and addition.

Your child learned:
- Phonetic recognition of beginning sounds.
- Addition.
- Identification of plus and minus signs.

To review what your child has learned, do the three activities below. If your child is having difficulty in any of the areas below, go back and review the pages with him or her. You can also review and reinforce the skills in this section with the additional activities listed below.

1. Tell your child to put an X in the blank before all of the words that have the same beginning sounds.

   _____cake _____cat _____string _____call _____blue

2. Have your child circle the word that has a different beginning sound than the others.

   duck   dance   dream   happy   dot

3. David has 4 red balloons and gets 2 blue balloons. Ask your child to draw a picture of David's balloons, and then write an addition number sentence to show how many balloons he has altogether.

Additional Activities
Below are some interactive ways you and your child can practice what you have worked on in this chapter. These activities will reinforce the skills your child studied on the previous pages.

1. Write a series of 3-4 words, with at least two of them having the same beginning sounds. See if your child can pick the words with the same beginning sounds.
2. Say three words out loud. See if your child can identify the word with the different beginning sound. Then reverse roles and have your child give you three words, one of which having a different beginning sound for you to identify.
3. Find objects in your home such as marbles, buttons, or blocks. Practice laying out objects for your child to add up to three. Practice making the plus and minus signs. Have your child count to three as he or she is picking up toys.

Chapter 18

Today's lesson will be lots of fun as we join Rosa and Paige as they get ready to plant seeds in their garden!

While they work, you will have a good time learning:
• Beginning sounds
• Number stories
• Coin identification

Now let's see what's happening in the garden!

Different Beginning Sounds

Color the picture whose name starts with a different sound than the others.

hat

horse

hut

car

Look carefully at each picture and say each word before you decide.

Different Beginning Sounds

Circle the word in each row that starts with a different sound than the others.

train   pen   truck

map   book   bus

fan   fox   leaf

Different Beginning Sounds

Rosa has been busy at the beach. Color the things with names that start with the **b** sound. Circle the things with names that start with a different sound.

Figuring Things Out

Read the following picture sentences and answer the questions below.

Sam saw  .

Then he saw  .

How many birds did Sam see?

Step 1: Count.  —————

Step 2: Count on.  —————

Sam saw ——— birds.

To **count on**, you add a number to each number you count.

Recognizing Coin Names

Draw a line from each coin on the ladybug to the leaf that names the coin.

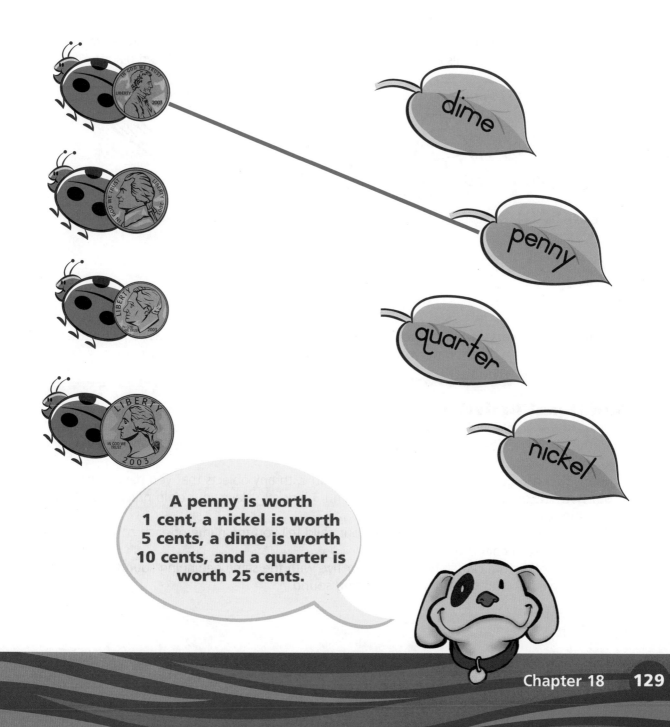

A penny is worth 1 cent, a nickel is worth 5 cents, a dime is worth 10 cents, and a quarter is worth 25 cents.

Assessment

Chapter 18 Review

In this chapter, your child studied beginning sounds, addition, and the names of coins. Because repetition is an effective method to reinforce learning, some exercises in this chapter were similar.

Your child learned:
- Discernment of different beginning sounds.
- Addition.
- Recognition of coins.

To review what your child has learned, do the activities below. Go back through the pages of this chapter with your child if he or she is having difficulty in any of the following areas. You can also review and reinforce the skills of this section with the additional activities listed below.

1. Ask your child to color the picture whose name starts with a different sound.

2. In each row below, have your child circle the word with the different beginning sound.

wall	truck	tooth	train

stop	sit	hat	sat

3. Susie has 2 toy cars and then finds 2 more toy cars. Tell your child to draw a picture that shows Susie's cars. Then, have your child use counting on to find out how many toy cars Susie has altogether.

Additional Activities

Here are some simple and fun activities you can do with your child to practice what you have worked on in this chapter. These activities will reinforce the skills your child studied on the previous pages.

1. Help your child practice addition by counting on with any objects that you have at home. Set out two sets of the object (such as blocks and 3 blocks). Have your child practice adding them together by counting on.
2. Grab a handful of loose change. Have your child tell you the name of each coin. You could ask how much each coin is worth.
3. Find a set of picture cards. Lay out four or five with the same beginning sound. Have your child find the picture with the different beginning sound.

Chapter 19

Today's lesson will be lots of fun as we join Paige and Sam as they swim in the pool!

While they frolic, you will have a good time learning:
- Ending sounds
- Coin value identification

Now let's see what's happening in the pool!

Ending Sounds: t

Find the pictures that end with the same sound as **bat**.
Draw a line to connect those pictures to the boat.

Say the word **bat**. Do you hear the **t** sound at the end of the word?

Ending Sounds: n

Say the name of each picture below. Color the pictures with names that end with the same sound as **sun.**

sun

Don't get a
sunbur**n**! Always
use sunscree**n**.

Ending Sounds: d

Circle the pictures that end with the letter **d**.

Good job!

Matching Coins to their Values

"Value" means how much the coin is worth.

Draw a line from each coin in the cloud to the raindrop that names the coin. Then draw a line from the name of each coin to the flower with the coin's value.

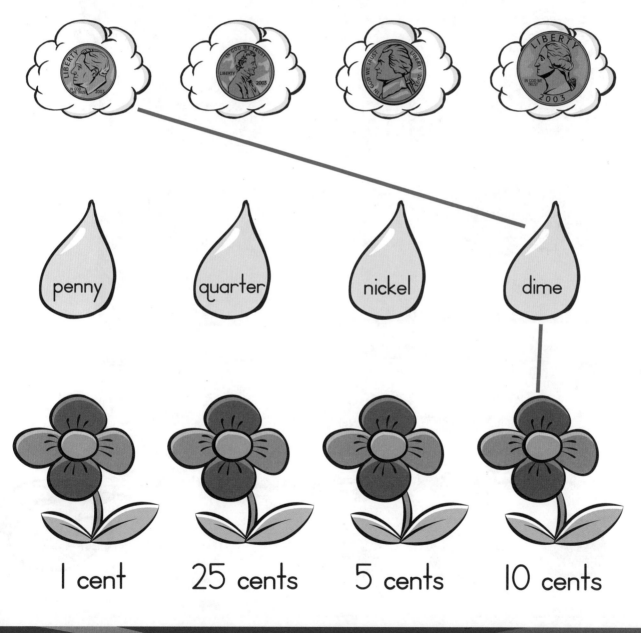

penny   quarter   nickel   dime

1 cent   25 cents   5 cents   10 cents

Finding Coins

Follow each coin through the garden. Then write the value of the coin you followed.

You found a lot of money!

_____   _____   _____

Assessment

Chapter 19 Review

In Chapter 19, your child studied ending sounds and coin names and values.

Your child learned:
- Recognition of the ending sound of the letters T, N, and D.
- Identification of coins.
- Recognition of numeric value of coins.

The following activities will allow your child to review the things studied in this chapter. If your child is having difficulty in any of the areas below, go review the pages of this chapter with your child. You can also review and reinforce the skills covered in this chapter with the additional activities at the bottom of this page.

1. Tell your child to circle the words that have this ending sound: t.

    ball   bat   fall   hat   one

2. Ask your child to circle the words that have this ending sound: n.

    hen   tin   fox   spoon   sit

3. Have your child match the picture of the coins in the first row to their names in the second row, and then match the names to their values in the third row:

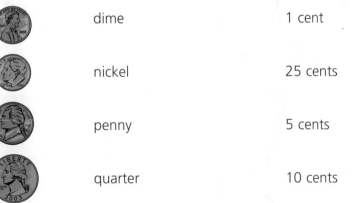

	dime	1 cent
	nickel	25 cents
	penny	5 cents
	quarter	10 cents

Additional Activities

Here are some simple and fun activities you can do with your child to practice what you have worked on in Chapter 19. These activities will reinforce the skills your child learned on the previous pages.

1. Go on a hunt with your child through your house in search of items that share the same ending sound (such as mat and hat, can and pen, and so on).
2. Spread some coins out on a table. As you point to one, have your child tell you the name of the coin and its value.

Chapter 20

Today's lesson will be lots of fun as we join Quincy as he teaches Paige and Marco in the classroom!

While they study, you will have a good time learning:
- Ending sounds
- Word problems
- Identification of time to the hour

Now let's see what's going on in the classroom!

Ending Sounds: m

Circle four pictures that end with the **m** sound.

Ending Sounds: p

Help Bogart get to the water. Connect the pictures that have the same ending sound as **cap.**

cap

STOP

START

Figuring Things Out

Rosa comes home from school and finds this note. It is 3:00 P.M.

She will have to spend one hour on each item on the list. Then she can play. At what time will Rosa get to play?

1. Do Homework
2. Do Chores
3. Eat Dinner

Step 1: Count on 1 hour.

1. Homework 3:00, _____

Step 2: Count on 1 hour.

2. Chores 4:00, _____

Step 3: Count on 1 hour.

3. Dinner 5:00, _____

Rosa may play at _____

To **count on,** you add 1 to the number you just counted.

Reading Clocks on the Hour

Draw a line from the clock on the left to the clock on the right that shows the same time.

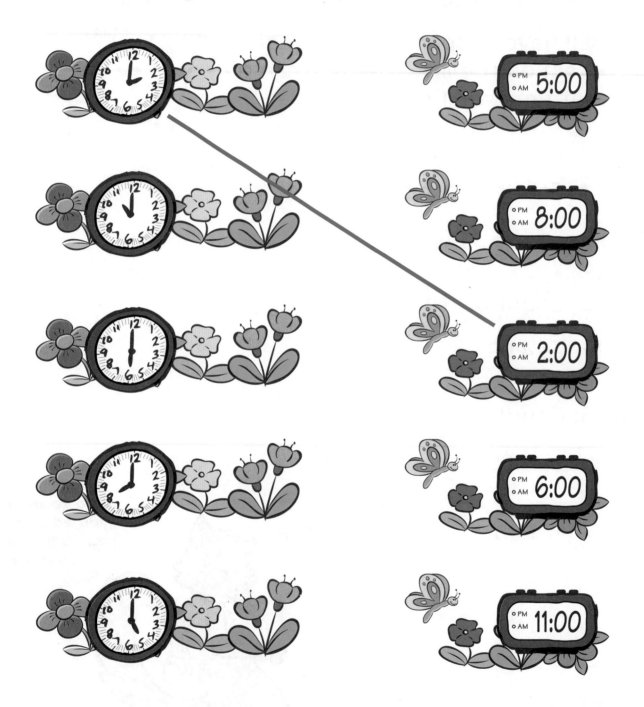

Drawing Clocks on the Hour

Draw hands on each clock to show the time.

1:00

7:00

10:00

9:00

3:00

12:00

I don't have much time left!

Filling in the Clock

Fill in the correct time on the clock, and fill in the dot for AM or PM.

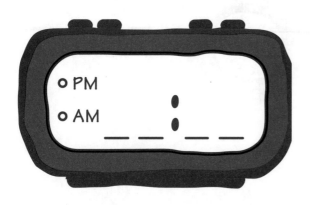

7:00 PM

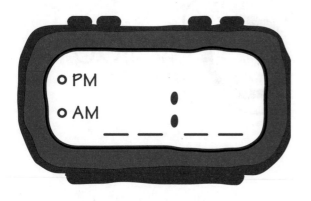

1:00 AM

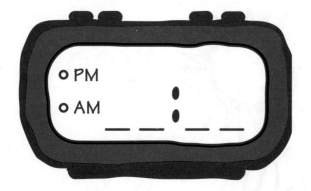

10:00 PM

Is it dinner time yet?

Chapter 20 Review

In this chapter, your child studied ending sounds and how to tell time.

Your child learned:
- Phonetic recognition of ending sounds M and P.
- Reading time on clocks to the hour.

Work with your child on the chapter review activities shown below. If your child has difficulty with any of these exercises, go back through the chapter with him or her to review the material. You can also review and reinforce these skills with your child using the exercises in the additional activities section below.

1. Have your child circle the words that end with the m sound:

mat   drum   arm   mad   pan   pat

2. Ask your child to underline the words that end with the p sound:

cap   mop   play   trap   six   bump

3. Draw a line to match the clocks on the left with the times on the right:

6:00

5:00

2:00

Additional Activities
Below are some interactive ways you and your child can review what you have worked on in this chapter. These activities will reinforce the skills your child studied on the previous pages.

1. Ask your child to think of as many words as possible that end with the "m" sound. Then do the same with the ending "p" sound.
2. Using a play clock, move the hands to show a time to the hour. See if your child can tell you what time it is.
3. Create a daily schedule together. Write times to the hour on your schedule and corresponding activities. As you move through the day, show your child how the clock matches the times and activities on your schedule. Ask questions like, "What are we going to do at 2:00?" or "What time do you have a snack?"

Chapter 21

Today's lesson will be lots of fun as we join everyone down on the farm!

While they explore, you will have a good time learning:
- Ending sounds
- Measuring
- The sequence of events

Now let's see what's happening down on the farm!

Ending Sounds: x

Underline the pictures that have the same ending sound as **fox.**

fo<u>x</u>

Being on this farm helps me rela**x**!

Ending Sounds: g

Draw a line from the pictures that end with the **g** sound to the big letter **g**.

frog

You're good at finding sounds in words!

Ending Sounds: l

Sam and Marco are going to play volleyball. They will play with anything that ends with the **l** sound! Cross out the pictures of the things Sam and Marco will <u>not</u> use in their game.

Ball ends with the **l** sound!

ba**ll**

Measuring Length to the Nearest Inch

Riddle: What kind of worm can measure?

To solve the riddle, first circle the measurement that matches the length of each object.

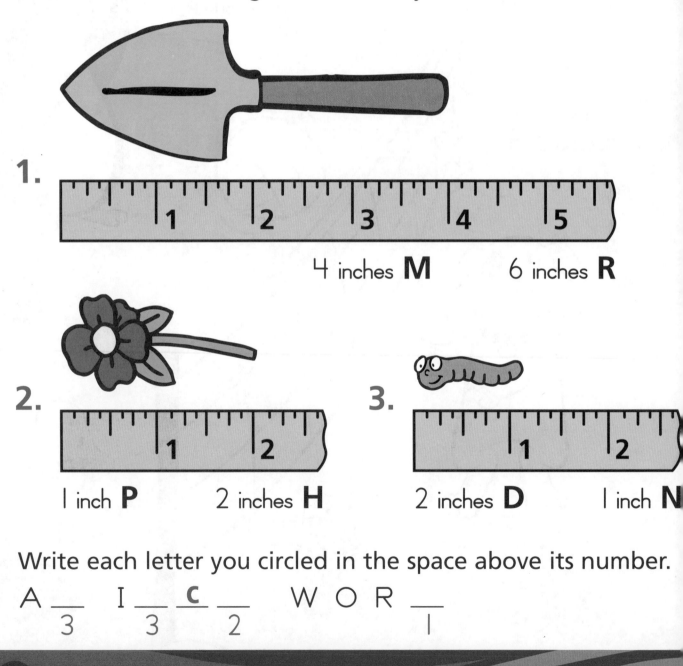

1.

4 inches **M**   6 inches **R**

2.

I inch **P**   2 inches **H**

3.

2 inches **D**   I inch **N**

Write each letter you circled in the space above its number.

A __ I __ **C** __ W O R __
  3   3 2   1

Sequencing Events

Number the order of the items.

Great job!

2   1   3

Assessment

Chapter 21 Review

Your child studied ending sounds, measurement, and sequencing in Chapter 21.

Your child learned:
- Phonetic recognition of the ending sounds of X, G, and L.
- Measurement in inches.
- How to order sets.

The following activities will provide a review of what your child has learned. If he or she has any difficulty in any of the areas below, go back through the pages of this chapter with your child. You can also review and reinforce the skills in this section with the additional activities listed below.

1. Ask your child to circle the words that have the same ending sound as dog:

peg   goat   tag   pat   grab   leg

2. Have your child cross out the words that do not end with x:

box   ball   net   six   fox   mix   pan

3. Help your child measure the following items to the nearest inch:

Your shoe: _____in.

A book: _____in.

Your toothbrush: _____in.

Additional Activities
Here are some simple and fun things you can do with your child to practice what you have worked on in this chapter. To help reinforce what was learned in this chapter, try these activities.

1. Brainstorm words that end with x, g, or l. Say some words out loud and ask, "What is the ending sound?"
2. Go on a "measure hunt." Have your child find as many things as possible that measure 1 inch, 2 inches, 3 inches, etc. Make a list of these objects.
3. Practice sequencing events. Find or draw a set of three pictures and have your child put them in order.

Chapter 22

Today's lesson will be lots of fun as we join Sam, Quincy, and Marco while they visit the beach.

While they explore, you will have a good time learning:
• Ending sounds
• The recognition of plane shapes

Now let's see what's going on at the beach!

Same Ending Sounds

Some words have washed up on the beach! Underline the two words that end with the same sound.

frog

net

cat

Listen to the ending sounds!

Same Ending Sounds

Look at the pictures below. Color the two pictures that have the same ending sound.

hat

Sam

cat

Finding Squares

Color the squares in the tree. A **square** has four sides of equal length.

A square looks like this: ■ .

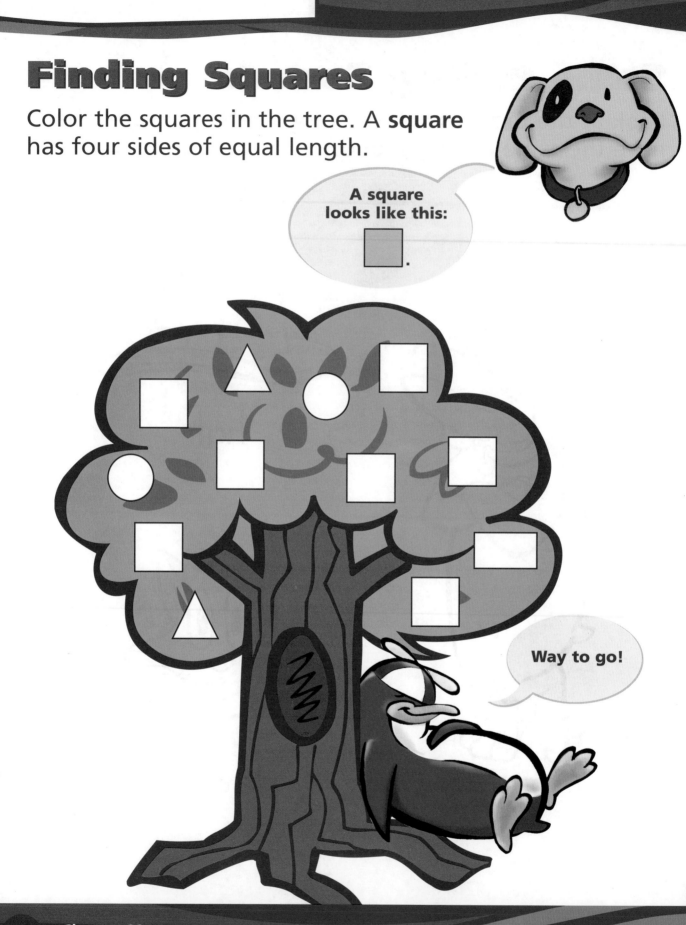

Way to go!

Finding Triangles

Draw a circle around each triangle on the tiger cub. A **triangle** has three sides.

A triangle
looks like this:

Drawing Triangles

Trace the triangles Bogart passes as he skates through the jungle maze.

Assessment

Chapter 22 Review

In this chapter, your child studied recognizing of ending sounds, how to identify shapes, and how to draw triangles..

Your child learned how to:
- Recognize same ending sounds.
- Identify squares and triangles.
- Draw triangles.

The following activities will allow your child to review the things studied in this chapter. If your child is having difficulty in any of the areas below, review the pages of this chapter with your child. You can also review and reinforce the skills covered in this chapter with the additional activities at the bottom of this page.

1. Have your child underline the words that have the same ending sound:

hat   kite   time   pan

2. Ask your child: How many triangles are there? _____

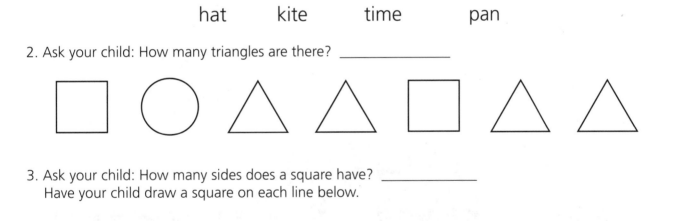

3. Ask your child: How many sides does a square have? _____
   Have your child draw a square on each line below.

_____   _____   _____

Additional Activities

Here are some simple and fun activities you can do with your child to practice what you have worked on in Chapter 22. These activities will reinforce the skills your child learned on the previous pages.

1. Cut out different shapes from colored contact paper. Let your child peel the back off and create shape pictures. Discuss the names of each shape and characteristics of each one.
2. With your child, make finger jello and use cookie cutters to cut jello into different shapes.
3. Have your child go on a shape hunt in his or her room. Tell your child to try to find objects shaped like circles, squares, and triangles.

Chapter 23

Today's lesson will be lots of fun as we join Rosa and Quincy while they soar high in the sky!

While they explore, you will have a good time learning:
• Ending sounds
• The recognition of plane shapes

Now let's see what's going on up in the sky!

Same Ending Sounds

Color the shells with pictures that have names ending with the same sound as **bug.**

bug

rug

apple

book

dog

pig

Different Ending Sounds

Find the word with the ending sound that doesn't belong. Then color the picture it names.

Tom

jam

gum

fox

Keep going!

Different Ending Sounds

Put an X on the things whose names end with a different sound than the one you hear in  sun.

moon

fish

pin

van

cat

grapes

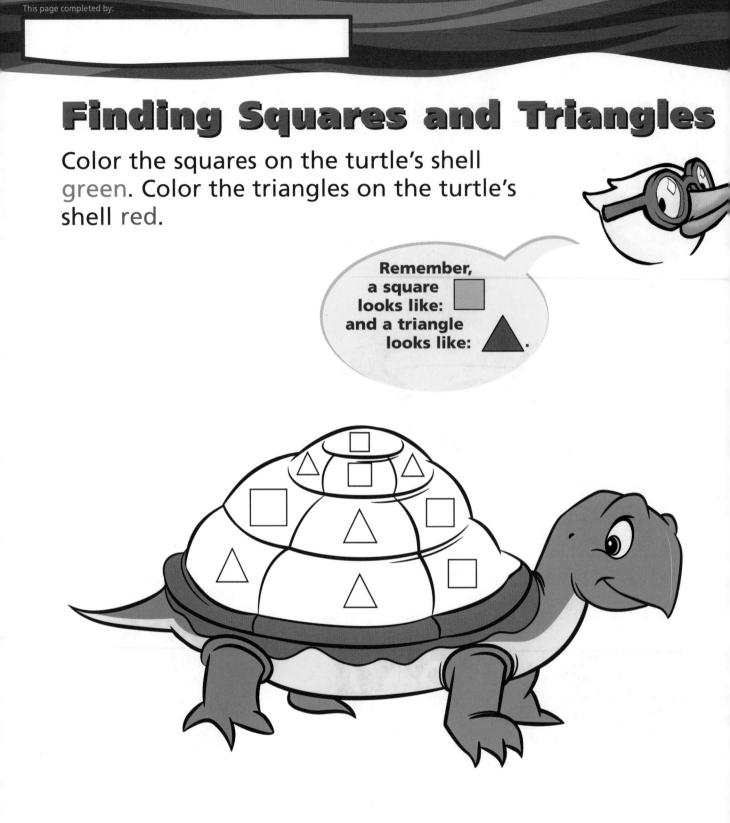

Finding Squares and Triangles

Color the squares on the turtle's shell green. Color the triangles on the turtle's shell red.

Remember, a square looks like: and a triangle looks like: .

Picturing Things

Rosa was looking through her telescope one night, and this is what she saw.

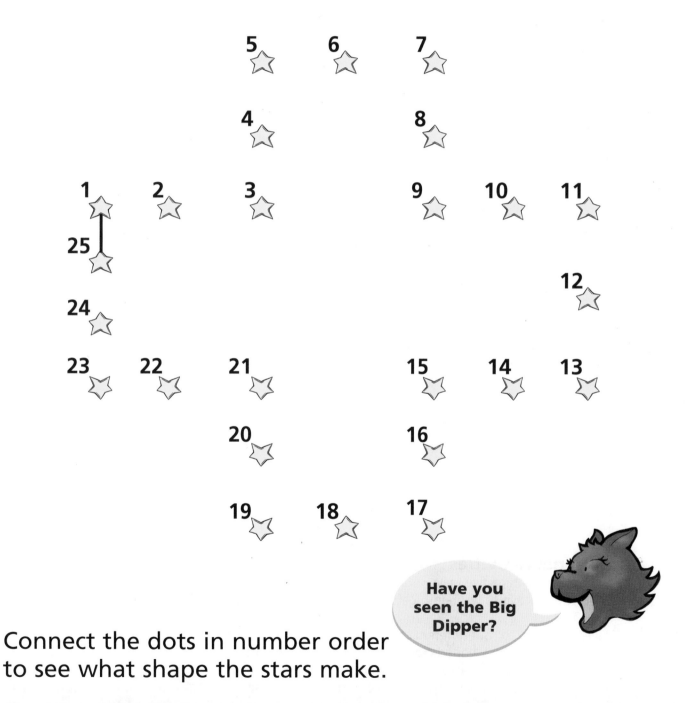

Have you seen the Big Dipper?

Connect the dots in number order to see what shape the stars make.

Assessment

Chapter 23 Review

In this chapter, some activities were repeated to reinforce your child's learning. Your child studied ending sounds and identifying shapes.

Your child learned:
- Recognition of same ending sounds.
- Differentiation of ending sounds.
- Identification of square and triangles.

Do the following activities to review what your child has learned. If your child is having difficulty in any of the areas below, go back through the pages of this chapter with your child. With the additional activities listed below, you can also review and reinforce the skills covered in this chapter.

1. Tell your child to circle the word that has a different ending sound.

pan   dog   jog   beg

2. Have your child underline the words that have the same ending sound as sit.

pet   fox   dog   bat   fast   egg

3. Ask your child: How many sides does a triangle have?_____
   In the space below, have your child draw five triangles.

Additional Activities
Below are some interactive ways you and your child can review what you have worked on in this chapter. These activities will reinforce the skills your child studied on the previous pages.

1. Have your child cut out different shapes and make shape-people or shape-animals.
2. Share some different-shaped crackers. Have your child sort them by shape first and tell the names of the shapes before he or she is allowed to eat them.
3. Help your child use cookie cutters to make squares and triangles out of clay. Make sculptures with the shapes.

Chapter 24

Today's lesson will be lots of fun as we join Bogart and Quincy while they explore the desert!

While they explore, you will have a good time learning:
- Rhyming words
- The identification of plane shapes

Now let's see what's going on in the desert!

Rhyming Words

Bogart finds two pictures on the cave wall! Say the name for each picture. Do you hear any sounds that repeat? Trace the sounds that are the same.

Words that have the same middle and ending sounds are called rhyming words.

cat

rat

Listen to the middle and ending sounds of words to see if they rhyme.

Rhyming Words

Come see what Paige found in the cave! The words under the pictures rhyme. Trace the rhyming sounds below.

Say the words out loud, and listen to that **-og** sound.

Finding Circles

Draw an X over the circles that you find.
Then color the picture.

A circle looks like: .

BEWARE!
Alligator Crossing

Finding Rectangles

A **rectangle** has four sides. Two of a rectangle's sides are the same length. How many rectangles can you help Rosa find on the safari van?

A rectangle looks like:

We found them!

There are _____ rectangles on the safari van.

Finding Circles and Rectangles

Color the circles on the snake purple. Color the rectangles on the snake yellow.

Remember, a circle looks like: ●, and a rectangle looks like: ▭.

Assessment

Chapter 24 Review

In this chapter, your child studied rhyming words and how to identify shapes. Because repetition is an effective method to reinforce learning, some exercises in this chapter were similar.

Your child learned:
- Recognition of rhyming words.
- Recognition of circles and rectangles.

The following activities will provide a review of what your child has learned. If he or she has any difficulty in any of the areas below, go back through the pages of this chapter with your child. You can also review and reinforce the skills in this section with the additional activities listed below.

1. Ask your child to draw a line to connect the pictures that rhyme.

2. Have your child do the following: List two items in your home that are the shape of a circle. List two items that are the shape of a rectangle.

   Circles _____ _____   Rectangles _____ _____

3. Have your child look at the picture on page 172. How many circles are on the snake? _____ How many rectangles are there? _____

Additional Activities
Below are some interactive ways you and your child can practice what you have worked on in this chapter. These activities will reinforce the skills your child studied on the previous pages.

1. Go on a walk and search for things that rhyme.
2. Look through a magazine and cut out circle shapes.
3. Name a shape. Have your child hunt for that shape around your home.

Chapter 25

Today's lesson will be lots of fun as we join Bogart while he helps on the farm!

While he explores, you will have a good time learning:
• Rhyming words
• Recognization of plane shapes
• Identification of plane shapes

Now let's see what's going on at the farm!

Rhyming Words

Say the name of each picture. Color the pictures with names that rhyme with **bat.**

Do you hear any words with the sound-at?

hat

box

mat

net

sat

top

Rhyming Words

Write the missing letters on the lines. You will find them in the box. Do the words rhyme?

o p

h _____

I know another
word that rhymes!
It's **mop!**

t _____

p _____

Drawing Trapezoids

Trace the trapezoids to help the gorilla find his home. Color the trapezoid that you think is big enough to be his home.

It's fun to say the word trapezoid!

This page completed by:

Chapter 25   177

Finding the Names of Shapes

Draw a line from each shape to its name.

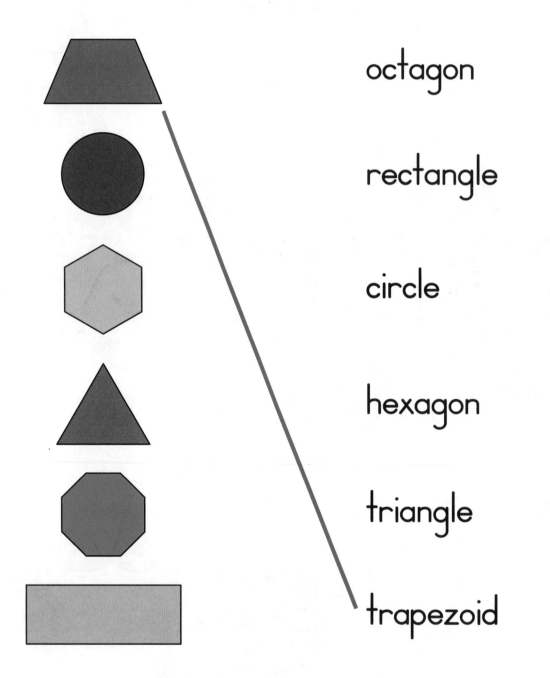

octagon

rectangle

circle

hexagon

triangle

trapezoid

Describing Combined Shapes

Circle the names of the shapes used.

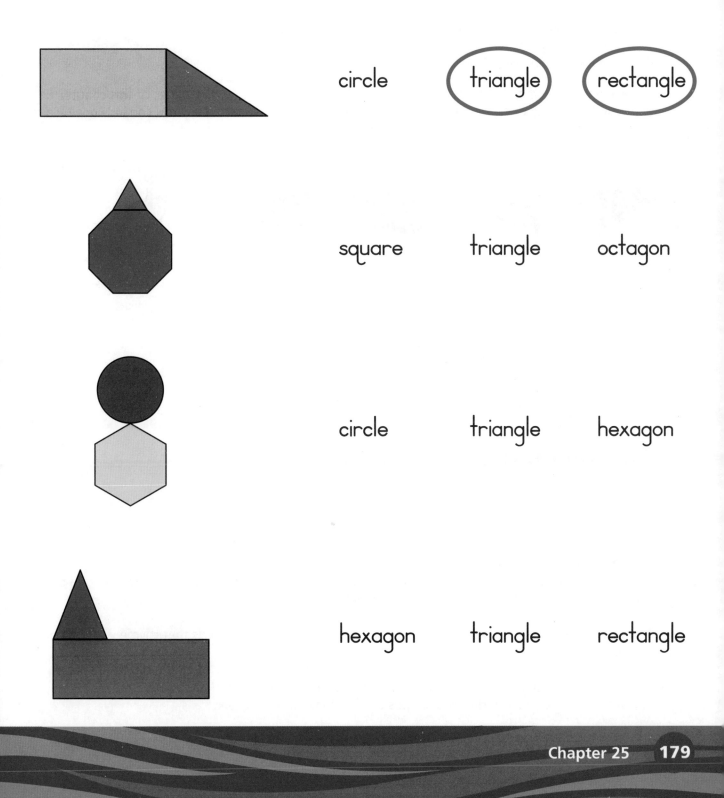

circle   (triangle)   (rectangle)

square   triangle   octagon

circle   triangle   hexagon

hexagon   triangle   rectangle

Assessment

Chapter 25 Review

In Chapter 25, your child studied rhyming words and identifying shapes.

Your child learned:
- Rhyming words.
- Recognition of shapes.

To review what your child has learned, do the activities below. Review the pages of this chapter with your child if he or she is having difficulty in any of the following areas. You can also review and reinforce the skills in this section with the additional activities listed below.

1. Have your child write the letters below that will make the words rhyme.

_____   _____   _____

2. Tell your child to color each hexagon blue and each trapezoid purple.

3. Ask your child the following questions:

What shape is a stop sign? _____
What shapes are in a traffic light? _____
What shapes are in a semi-truck? _____

Additional Activities
Below are some interactive ways you and your child can practice what you have worked on in this chapter. These activities will reinforce the skills your child studied on the previous pages.

1. Use the words bay and hot. Have your child make a list of all the words that rhyme with bay or hot. Use your own ideas for other words.
2. Go to the park and go on a shape hunt. Help your child make a list of all the different shapes you see. Have your child draw a picture of where the shapes were found.
3. Have your child practice drawing shapes on the sidewalk with chalk.

Chapter 26

Today's lesson will be lots of fun as we join Paige and Quincy while they explore the woods!

While they explore, you will have a good time learning:
- Rhyming words
- Patterns

Now let's see what's going on in the woods!

Rhyming Words

Sam found an interesting old pot in the cave.
Circle the pictures with names that rhyme with **pot.**

bat

top

dot

I like rhymes
a **lot!**

cot

net

pup

Rhyming Words

What does Marco see in the cave? Write the missing letters on the lines. The ones you need are in the box. Do the words rhyme?

u p

Remember to say the words out loud.

p _____

_____

c _____

Rhyming Words

Paige is having fun having a tea party. Circle the words that rhyme with **fun.**

sun

ham

bun

bed

top

run

Recognizing Patterns of Shapes

Follow this pattern ◯◯▢ through the jungle so the monkey can eat the banana. You can move over, down, or diagonally. Color the pattern purple.

Talking About Things

Play this game with a friend.

Say a sound pattern and have your friend repeat it.

For example, say, "Ooga, Bam, Bam, Ooga." Your friend will repeat, "Ooga, Bam, Bam, Ooga."

Then have your friend say a sound pattern, such as, "Ta Da Ta, Ta Da Ta." Then you will repeat, "Ta Da Ta, Ta Da Ta."

See how long you both can play without making a mistake!

Assessment

Chapter 26 Review

Your child studied rhyming words and the identification of shapes in Chapter 26.

Your child learned:
- Recognition of rhyming words.
- Recognition of patterns of shapes.

To review what your child has learned, do the three activities below. If your child is having difficulty in any of the following areas, go back and review the pages with him or her. You can also review and reinforce the skills in this section with the additional activities listed below.

1. Tell your child to finish the words below by writing a word that rhymes with "net."

    w _ _   g _ _   s _ _   b _ _

2. Have your child draw the shapes to make this pattern: triangle, circle, and rectangle. Have him or her repeat the pattern three times.

    — — —   — — —   — — —

3. Direct your child to create his or her own pattern using these shapes: Repeat your pattern three times.

    — — — — — — — — —

Additional Activities

Do the following activities to review what your child has learned. If your child is having difficulty in any of the areas below, go back through the pages of this chapter with your child.

1. Draw shapes on the ground with chalk. Tell your child a pattern using the shapes. Have your child hop to the shapes to show the pattern.
2. Ask your child to think of the names of children he or she knows. Discuss if there are words that rhyme with any of his friends' names.
3. Look in magazines or on a walk. Hunt for patterns of shapes.

Chapter 27

Today's lesson will be lots of fun as we join Marco and Bogart while they explore the garden!

While they explore, you will have a good time learning:
- High-frequency words
- Patterns

Now let's see what's going on in the garden!

Sight Words

Here is the swamp! Say the word **the** out loud. Then trace the word **the** below.

the

swamp

Sight Words

Circle the word **the** each time you find it in the picture.

the bird

the leaf

the frog

the tree

the flowers

Picturing Things

Find the patterns that are alike in each set below.
Color the objects that are alike in each pattern
the same color.

1.

2.

3.

Extending Patterns of Size

This set of trees has a pattern. Draw a line from each tree at the bottom of the page to the empty square that shows its place in the pattern.

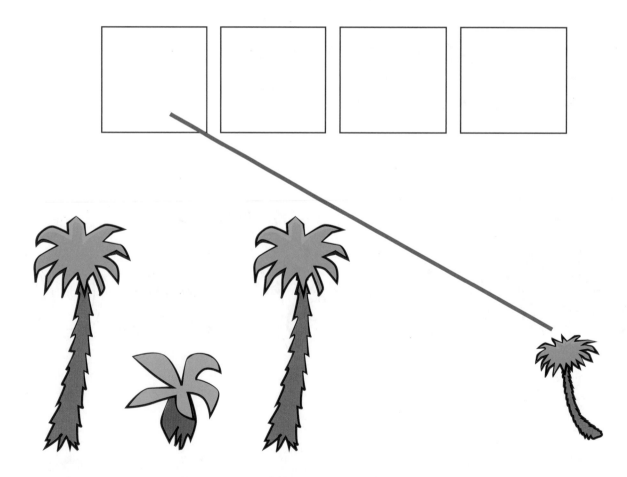

Sight words: "the"

Complete the sentence by writing the word "the" in each line. Read the sentence aloud.

___ cat ran away
from ___ dog.

This is fun!

Assessment

Chapter 27 Review

In this chapter, your child studied sight words and patterns. Because repetition is an effective method to reinforce learning, some exercises in this chapter were similar.

Your child learned:
- Recognition of sight words.
- Identification of patterns.
- Extension of patterns of size.

To review what your child has learned, do the three activities below. If your child is having difficulty in any of the areas below, go back and review the pages with him or her. You can also review and reinforce the skills in this section with the additional activities listed below.

1. In the following sentence, tell your child to make a square around the word **the** each time he or she sees it.

   The cat and the dog and the boy went to the lake to catch the fish.

2. Have your child do the following:
   Continue this pattern of size using squares. Repeat it two times.

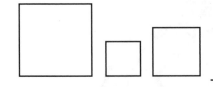 _____ _____ _____ _____ _____ _____

3. Ask your child to write the word **the** in front of each word. Have your child read each phrase out loud.

   _____ dog   _____ cat   _____ mom   _____ dad

Additional Activities

Here are some interactive ways you and your child can practice what you have worked on in this chapter. These activities will reinforce the skills your child studied on the previous pages.

1. Using the word **the**, have your child write labels for items around your home.
2. Gather several pairs of shoes. Have your child use the shoes to create patterns of size.
3. While reading a favorite story, have your child point out the word **the** as you read.

Chapter 28

Today's lesson will be lots of fun as we join Paige and Marco while they explore the jungle!

While they explore, you will have a good time learning:
• Sentence completion
• Shape patterns
• Data collection

Now let's see what's going on in the jungle!

Sentences

Read what the robot is saying. Then complete the sentences by writing the word **is** on each line.

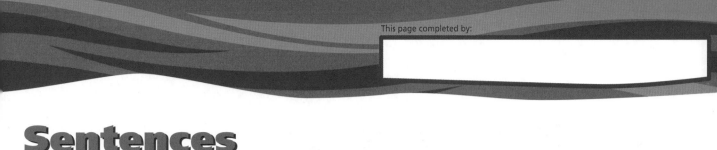

Sentences

Next, Marco and our friends go to Rainbow Planet.
Write the word with the matching color to complete
each sentence.

| yellow | green | blue | purple |

cat

dog

fox

bat

It is a blue _____ .

Is it a green _____ ?

It is a purple _____ .

Is it a yellow _____ ?

Creating Patterns of Shape

Let's make a jungle necklace!

Draw different shapes on the string below.

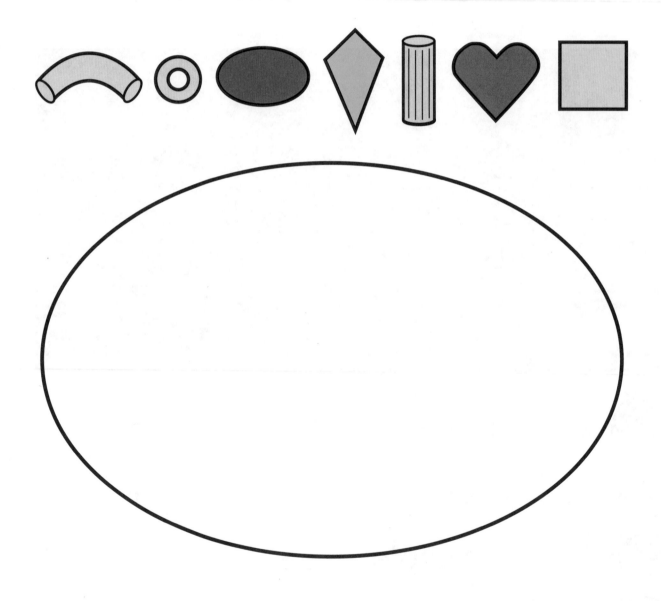

Gathering Information

Tell us about yourself.

Color the circle with your favorite color:

How many people are in your family? _____

Draw a picture of your family.

Write your age. _____

Color the fruit you like best.

Gathering Information

Find out things about other people.

Ask three people which of these colors they like best.

Name _____   Color _____

Name _____   Color _____

Name _____   Color _____

Ask four people whether they have one of these pets.

Name _____   Pet _____

Name _____   Pet _____

Name _____   Pet _____

Name _____   Pet _____

It's fun to learn about other people!

Assessment

Chapter 28 Review

Your child studied sentence completion, pattern identification, and data collection in Chapter 28.

Your child learned how to:
- Write mechanics.
- Create shape patterns.
- Gather Information.

Do the following activities to review what your child has learned. If your child is having difficulty in any of the following areas, go back through the pages of this chapter with your child. You can also review and reinforce the skills in this section with the additional activities listed below.

1. Have your child use the word **is** to complete the sentences, and write the answer to each question on the line.

What _____ your age? _____

What _____ your favorite food? _____

What _____ the name of your school? _____

2. Tell your child to write the color word to complete each sentence.

A stop sign is _____.

A ripe banana is _____.

The sky is _____.

3. Direct your child to draw this pattern: heart, diamond, diamond, square, heart, diamond, diamond, and square.

___ ___ ___ ___ ___ ___ ___ ___

Additional Activities
Here are some simple and fun activities you can do with your child to practice what you have worked on in this chapter. These activities will reinforce the skills your child studied on the previous pages.

1. Have your child come up with a few questions to ask the family each night at dinner.
2. Use utensils, plates, and cups to make patterns. Then have your child set the table.
3. While reading a story, ask your child questions about the illustrations.

Chapter 29

Today's lesson will be lots of fun as we join Sam and Rosa while they go to the movies!

While we watch the movie, you will have a good time learning how to:
- Follow directions
- Discriminate visually
- Begin probability

Now let's see what's going on at the movies!

Understanding Directions

The blue square is **above** the red circle.

Color the object **above** each penguin.

When one object is **above** another object, that object appears to be higher on the page.

Which Weighs More?

Circle the object on each scale that weighs **more**.

How much do you weigh?

Is it Possible or Impossible?

Answer each question by circling either YES or NO.

Is it possible to land on yellow?
YES   NO

Is it possible to land on blue?
YES   NO

Is it possible to land on green?
YES   NO

Is it possible to land on red?
YES   NO

Swell job!

Which Weighs More?

Circle the picture in each group that weighs the most.

Find the Hidden Picture

Follow the directions below to discover the hidden picture.

Color the stars yellow.
Color the "X" red.
Color the squares green.

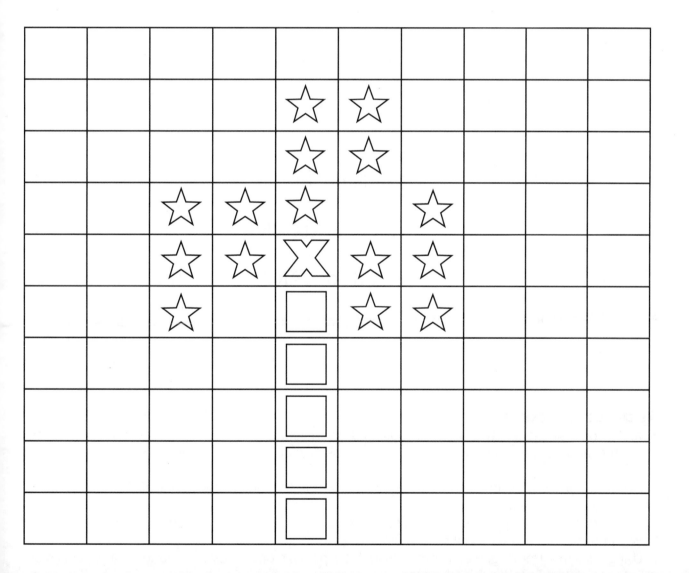

Assessment

Chapter 29 Review

In this chapter, your child studied how to follow directions and compare weights.

Your child learned:
- Comprehension of 2 and 3-step directions.
- Recognition of weight differences of objects.

To review what your child has learned, do the three activities below. If your child is having difficulty in any of the following areas, go back and review the pages with him or her. You can also review and reinforce the skills in this section with the additional activities listed below.

1. Tell your child to circle the pair of numbers where the 4 is above the 3.

4   4   4   3

3   2   3   4

2. Ask your child to tell you which weighs more.

CHAIR or SHIRT

BOOK or BALLOON

PENCIL or CAR

3. Have your child put a star above all of the 2s.

1   2   1   2   1

Additional Activities

Here are some simple and fun activities you can do with your child to practice what you have worked on in this chapter. These activities will reinforce the skills your child studied on the previous pages.

1. Ask your child who he or she thinks weighs the most in the family. Use your scale to see if your child guessed correctly.
2. Using your family scale or a small food scale, let your child collect items from around the house and weigh them to see what weighs the most.
3. Using a spinner from a game, ask your child if it is possible or impossible to land on a certain color. Let your child spin to discover the answer.

Chapter 30

Today's lesson will be lots of fun as we join Bogart and Marco while they go into outer space!

While they explore outer space, you will have a good time learning:
- High-frequency words
- Multi-step directions
- Cardinal directions

Now let's see what's going on in outer space!

Sight Words

Help Quincy with his Swamp Notebook by writing the word **a** on each line below.

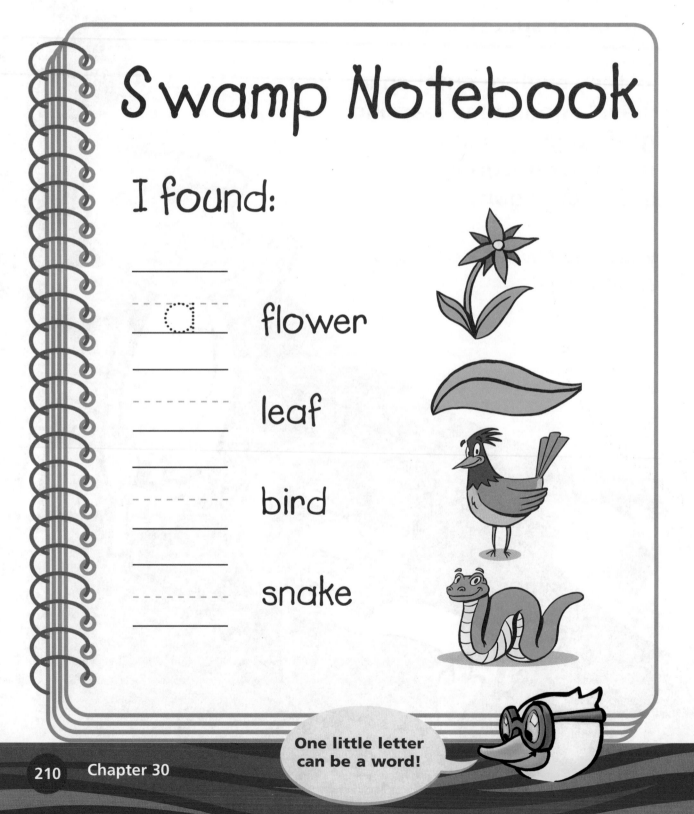

Swamp Notebook

I found:

_____ a _____ flower

_____ leaf

_____ bird

_____ snake

One little letter can be a word!

Sight Words

Look at all these books about swamp animals! Color the books with titles that have the word **and.**

Birds and Fish

Snakes and Turtles

Alligators

Butterflies

Lizards and Frogs

Sight Words

Help Marco find out who is in the swamp.
Circle the word I each time you find it in the picture.

Great job!

Understanding Directions

The red circle is **below** the blue square.

Find out who lives in each igloo by circling the animal **below** each igloo.

An object that is **below** another object appears lower on the page.

Understanding Directions

When a person is facing North, the side that is to his or her East is the right side.

North

West ← → East
Right

South

The 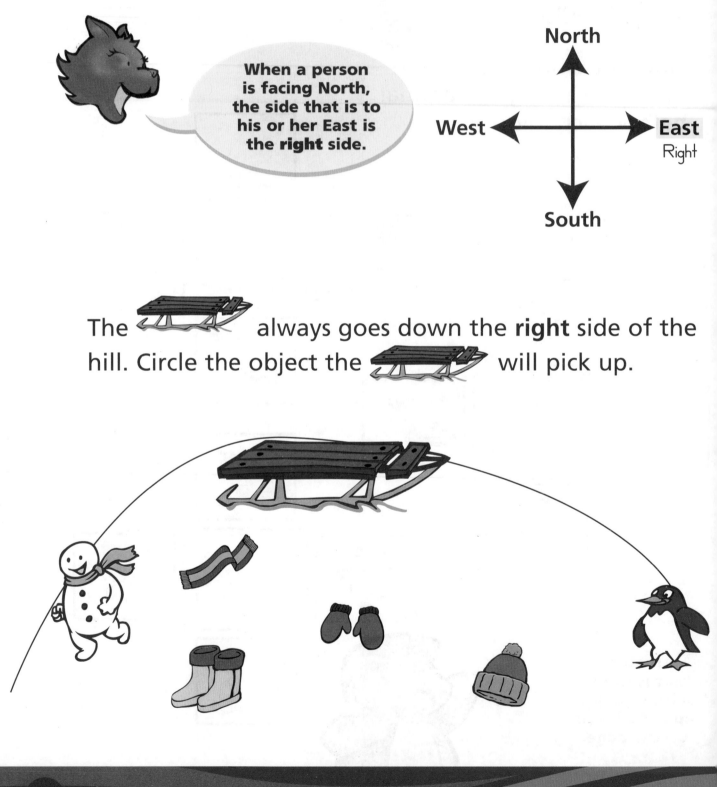 always goes down the **right** side of the hill. Circle the object the will pick up.

Assessment

Chapter 30 Review

In Chapter 30, your child studied sight words and directions.

Your child learned how to:
- Recognize sight words: a, i and and.
- Write lowercase "a."
- Comprehend the meaning of the word "below."
- Comprehend directions.

To review what your child has learned, do the activities below. Review the pages of this chapter with your child if he or she is having difficulty in any of the following areas. You can also review and reinforce the skills in this section with the additional activities listed below.

1. Have your child circle the words *a*, *i*, and *and* in these sentences:

I like butterflies and flowers.

We are reading a book.

2. Ask your child to circle the pair of numbers where the 4 is below the 3.

4   4   3   4
3   2   4   3

3. Ask your child which direction is on his or her right when he or she is facing North.

Additional Activities
Below are some interactive ways you and your child can practice what you have worked on in this chapter. These activities will reinforce the skills your child studied on the previous pages.

1. Using index cards, have your child make flash cards by writing "a" on one, "I" on another, and "and" on the last one. Ask your child to tell you a short story and hold up each card when he or she says that word.
2. Ask your child to gather five small objects from around the house (such as a marble, coin, game piece, and so on). Lay them out randomly on top of the squares on page 213. Then have your child point out which item is below each object. By changing the items around, you can do this several times with your child.
3. Find a map of your local community and, with your child, mark where you live. Using the map, have you child show you what area is to the East (right) of where you live.

Chapter 31

Today's lesson will be lots of fun as we join Sam and Bogart while they go outside to play!

While they explore outside, you will have a good time learning how to:
• Recognize high-frequency words
• Identify left and right
• Follow written directions

Now let's see what's going on outside!

PLAYHOUSE

Sight Words

What is in Sam's collection? Circle the word **my** wherever you find it below.

apple

my twig

my flower

my rock

bike

My leaf!

Sight Words

Write the word **is** on each line below to help Quincy with his swamp collection.

The rock _____is_____ in the box.

The leaf _____ in the box.

The flower _____ in the box.

The twig _____ in the box.

Sight Words

Look at the pictures Bogart and Marco sent home to friends. Draw a picture of yourself in the box and write the word **me** under it.

me

me

Telling Right and Left Apart

Color the object to the **left** of the South Pole blue.
Color the object to the **right** of the South Pole red.

Draw a pair of mittens to the **left** of Sam.
Draw a hat to the **right** of Sam.

Remember, when a person is facing North, **West** is to your **left** and East is to your **right**!

Understanding Directions

Color the object to the **left** of the snowman red.

Color the object **above** the snowman blue.

Color the object to the **right** of the snowman yellow.

Color the object **below** the snowman orange.

Assessment

Chapter 31 Review

Your child studied sight words, left and right, and directions in Chapter 31.

Your child learned:
- Comprehension of 4-step directions.
- Recognition of sight words: my, is, and me.
- Comprehsion of the placement of objects in relationship to other objects.

Do the following activities to review what your child has learned. If your child is having difficulty in any of the areas below, go back through the pages of this chapter with your child. You can also review and reinforce the skills in this section with the additional activities listed below.

1. Have your child circle the word to the left of the ☆ and draw a box around the word to the right of the ☆.

is ☆ my

2. Ask your child to write the word "my" in the blanks and then read the sentences to you.

The rock is in _____ box.

The leaf is in _____ box.

The apple is in _____ box.

3. Tell your child to circle the word "is" in the above sentences.

Additional Activities
Here are some interactive ways you and your child can practice what you have worked on in this chapter. These activities will reinforce the skills your child studied on the previous pages.

1. For several days to one week, have your child alternate which shoe she or he puts on first.
2. Using a table and an object of your child's choosing (marble, small toy), ask her or him to place the object below, to the right, above, and to the left of the table.
3. Using index cards, help your child make flash cards for the sight words "my," "is," and "me." Ask your child to tell you a short story and hold up each card when he or she says that word.

Chapter 32

Today's lesson will be lots of fun as we join Sam while he zooms around an alien planet in a flying saucer!

While he explores outer space, you will have a good time learning how to:
• Recognize sight words
• Follow written directions
• Recognize direction words in text

Now let's see what's going on in outer space!

Text Direction

Look at the direction in which Bogart is pointing.
Trace the arrows going left to right.

1. I can go to Sam.

2. Can you go to Sam?

3. Can you walk to the spaceship?

Text Direction

Now draw your own arrows.

4. I can walk to the star.
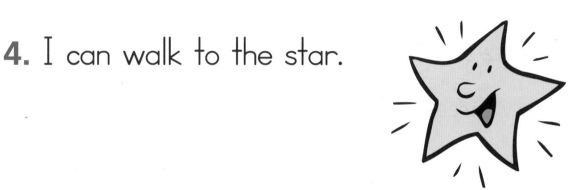

5. Can you go to the planet?

6. Can you get back to Earth?

Understanding Directions

Draw a cloud **above** the penguin.

Draw a sled **below** the penguin.

Draw a snowman to the **right** of the penguin.

Draw three snowflakes to the **left** of the penguin.

Remember, **above** is the opposite of **below**, and **left** is the opposite of **right**.

Understanding Directions

Circle the arrows pointing **left**.

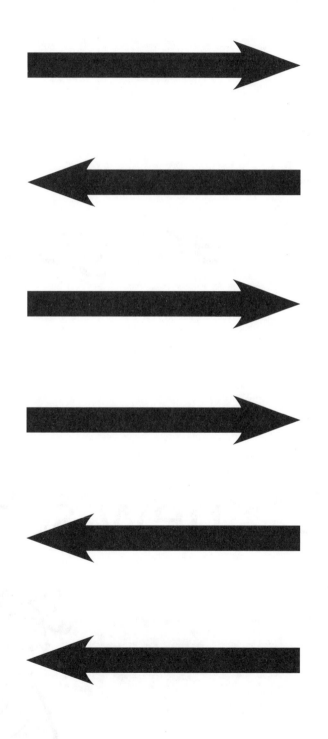

Sight Words "a" and "I"

Using the sight words "a" and "I," complete the sentence below. Read it aloud.

I
_____
- - - - - am going to

a
_____
- - - - - new school.

Great job!

Assessment

Chapter 32 Review

In this chapter, some activities were repeated to reinforce your child's learning. Your child studied directions, opposites, and sight words.

Your child learned:
- Recognition of text direction.
- Comprehension of directional orientation.
- Recognition of sight words: a and I.

To review what your child has learned, do the activities below. Go back through the pages of this chapter with your child if he or she is having difficulty in any of the following areas. You can also review and reinforce the skills of this section with the additional activities listed below.

1. Using the sight words "I" and "a," have your child complete this sentence:

_____ put _____bug in the box.

2. Ask your child to draw an arrow going left-to-right connecting the dots above the 1 and the 2.

•

1   2

3. Have your child:

- Put an "L" to the left of the star.
- Put an "R" to the right of the star.
- Put a "B" below the star.
- Put an "A" above the star.

Additional Activities
Here are some simple and fun things you can do with your child to practice what you have worked on in this chapter. To help reinforce what was learned in this chapter, try these activities.

1. Read a favorite story to your child and use your finger to illustrate that you are reading the words left-to-right.
2. Make up sentences using the sight words "a," "I," "and," "my," "is," and "me." Using the sight words flash cards you and your child made in Chapters 30 and 31, have your child hold up the flash card of the sight word you used.

Chapter 33

Today's lesson will be lots
of fun as we join Quincy,
Paige, and all their friends
while they investigate
a new treehouse!

While they explore, you
will have a good time learning:
• Letters with lines
• Word identification
• Pairs

Now let's see
what's going on
in the playhouse!

Identifying Letters

Circle the letters below that use only straight lines and no curves.

B Y R T M O

Q S N E I

A C D F G H

J K L P U

V W X Z

You've got it!

Identifying Letters

Write the uppercase letters with only straight lines.

___ ___ ___ ___ ___ ___

___ ___ ___ ___ ___

___ ___ ___

This is easy for you!

Lunch Letters

Identify words that begin with letters that have straight lines.

A _____   E _____

F _____   H _____

I _____   K _____

L _____   M _____

N _____   T _____

V _____   W _____

X _____   Y _____

Z _____

Nice work!

Pairs: Groups of Two

Circle the items below that are pairs.

I have some of those!

Pairs: Groups of Two

Draw a picture to complete the pair.

Assessment

Chapter 33 Review

In this chapter, your child studied letter identification and groups of two.

Your child learned:
- Comprehension of use of straight and curved lines when writing letters.
- Recognition of pairs.

To review what your child has learned, do the activities below. Review the pages of this chapter with your child if he or she is having difficulty in any of the following areas. You can also review and reinforce the skills in this section with the additional activities listed below.

1. Ask your child to circle the letters that only have straight lines.

Z   U   A   K   S

2. Have your child identify which of the items below come in pairs.

ears   shoes   hats   mittens

3. Ask your child to name something that comes in a pair and have him or her draw the items.

Additional Activities
Below are some interactive ways you and your child can review what you have worked on in this chapter. These activities will reinforce the skills your child studied on the previous pages.

1. Help your child write out the alphabet and then have her or him identify all of the letters that only have straight lines.
2. In one minute, see how many items you and your child can name that come in pairs.
3. When driving in the car, ask your child to identify letters on the road signs that only have straight lines.

Chapter 34

Today's lesson will be lots of fun as we join Marco and Bogart as they go to the movies!

While they are at the theater, you will have a good time learning how to:
- Recognize letters with curves
- Identify words
- Sequence
- Match

Now let's see what's going on at the movies!

THEATER

Identifying Letters

Circle the letters below that use both curved and straight lines.

B Y R T M O

Q S N E I

A C D F G H

J K L P U

V W X Z

Let me know
if you need
some help!

Identifying Letters

Identify the uppercase letters with curves.

____ ____ ____ ____ ____ ____

____ ____ ____ ____ ____

This is fun!

Starting Letters

Identify words that begin with letters that have curved lines.

B _____

C _____

D _____

G _____

J _____

O _____

P _____

Q _____

R _____

S _____

U _____

I'm trying to remember some too!

Who's Next

Draw a picture of the child who would come next.

Who's the match?

Draw a line to connect the matching people.

Assessment

Chapter 34 Review

In Chapter 34, your child studied letter recognition, matching, and patterns.

Your child learned:
- Comprehension of use of straight and curved lines when writing letters.
- Comprehension of event sequences.
- Attention to detail.

Do the following activities to review what your child has learned. If your child is having difficulty in any of the following areas, go back through the pages of this chapter with your child. With the additional activities listed below, you can also review and reinforce the skills covered in this chapter.

1. Ask your child which letter would come next.

A   B   A   B   ___

2. Have your child circle the letters that have curves.

S   A   Z   O   C

3. Have your child circle the letters that have both curved and straight lines.

B   A   K   R   H

Additional Activities

Here are some simple and fun activities you can do with your child to practice what you have worked on in Chapter 34. These activities will reinforce the skills your child learned on the previous pages.

1. Help your child write out the alphabet and then have her or him identify all of the letters that only have curved lines. Then identify all of the letters that have both curved and straight lines.
2. With your child, cut out squares of construction paper of different colors. Start a color pattern and ask your child to continue the pattern.
3. Play a game of "I Spy." (Give your child one clue at a time of something you both can see until your child determines what it is you're describing.)

Chapter 35

Today's lesson will be lots of fun as we join Quincy and Marco as they visit all their animal pals at the zoo!

While they explore the zoo, you will have a good time learning:
• Alphabetical order
• Letters
• Sequencing

Now let's see what's happening at the zoo!

Alphabetical Order

Place the food in alphabetical order using the first letter of each food item.

_____   _____

_____   _____

_____

Animal Book

You can be an author and illustrator of your own book. Each square will contain a picture of an animal beginning with that letter. Once you have drawn the picture and written the animal's name, have an adult help you cut out the box and begin to put your book together. Let's begin with letters A, B, C, D, E, and F.

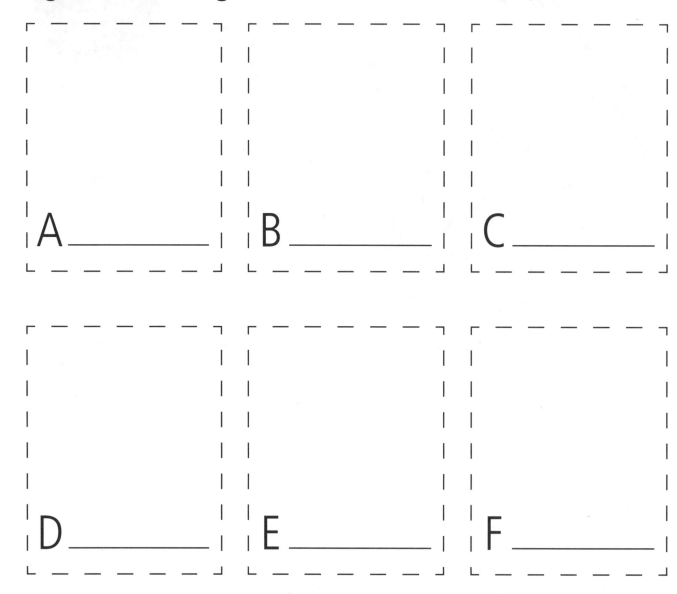

A_____   B_____   C_____

D_____   E_____   F_____

Who's the Match?

Draw a line to connect the matching people.

Beginning Sounds

Draw a line from the letter to the group of items that correspond with the beginning sound.

F

C

B

What's Next

Circle the picture that would come next.

What's Next?

a. b. c.

Assessment

Chapter 35 Review

Your child studied alphabetical order, phonetics, matching, and sequencing in Chapter 35.

Your child learned:
- Recognition of event sequences.
- Recognition of beginning letter sounds.
- Visual discernment and identification of pairs.

To review what your child has learned, do the two activities below. If your child is having difficulty in any of the following areas, go back and review the pages with him or her. You can also review and reinforce the skills in this section with the additional activities listed below.

1. Have your child put the letters below in alphabetical order:

E   C   B   D   A

2. Have your child draw a line from the letter to the food that corresponds with the beginning sound.

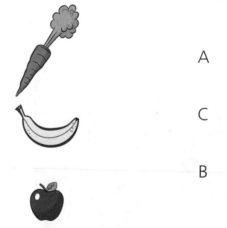

A

C

B

Additional Activities
Here are some simple and fun activities you can do with your child to practice what you have worked on in this chapter. These activities will reinforce the skills your child studied on the previous pages.

1. Using index cards, help your child make a flash card for each letter of the alphabet using both upper and lower case.
2. Help your child cut out pictures from magazines for each letter of the alphabet and glue each picture to the back of that letter's index card. For example: a picture of a car glued to the back of the index card for "Cc."
3. You can play many games with your child using these flash cards. Some game ideas are:
   - Pull out 5 cards and ask your child to put them in alphabetical order.
   - Show your child the picture side of the flash card and ask her or him to tell you the beginning letter of the picture.
   - Pick a card and have your child think of five words that begin with that letter.

Chapter 36

Today's lesson will be lots of fun. Let's join Marco as he dives deep under the water to a coral reef!

While he explores, you will have a good time learning:
- Sight words
- Number words

Now let's see what's happening in the ocean!

Animal Book

Keep working on your animal book. Draw a picture of an animal that begins with G, H, I, J, K, and L. Once you have drawn the pictures and written the animal's name in the space at the boxes bottom, have an adult help you cut the boxes out of the page and add them to your book.

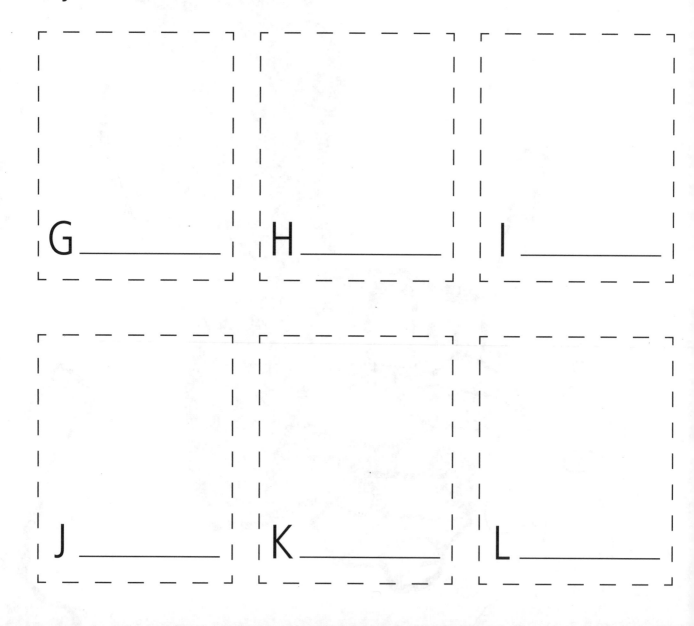

G_____   H_____   I_____

J_____   K_____   L_____

Beginning Sounds

Draw a line from the letter to the group of items that correspond with the beginning sound.

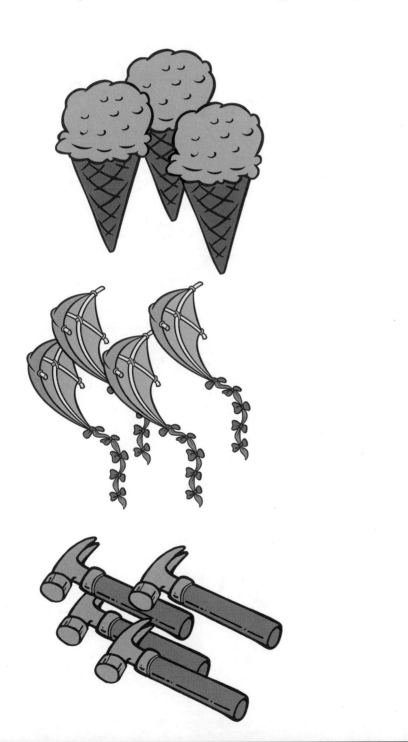

H

I

K

Sight Word Toss

Toss a penny onto one of the circled words below. Say the word aloud. Then put an "X" on the word after you say it.

Number Words

Complete the sentences below by filling in the missing number words.

I spy _____ tree.

I spy _____ flowers.

I spy _____ children.

I spy _____ footballs.

I spy _____ dogs.

You're doing so well!

Number Words

Write the number words on the line below the apple pictures.

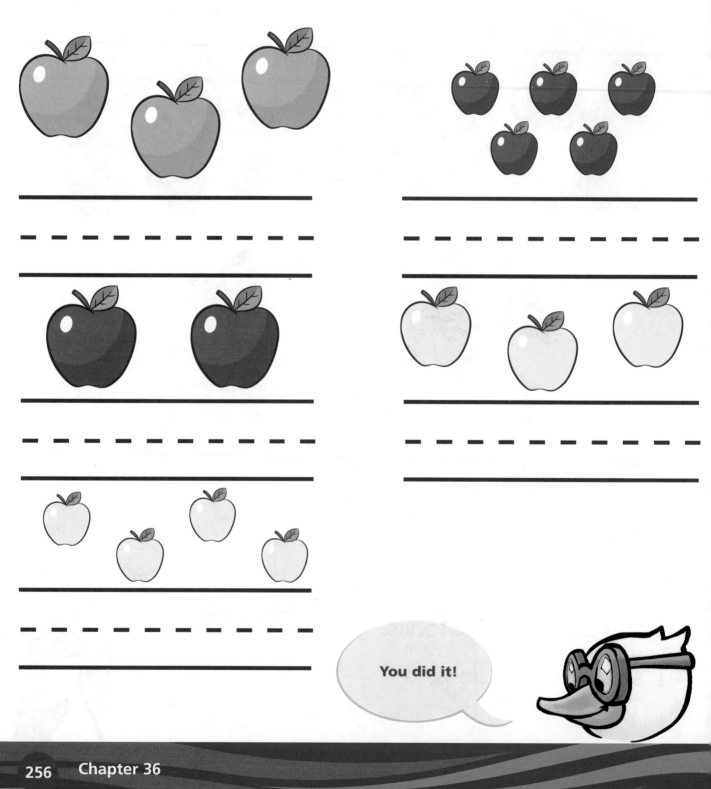

You did it!

Assessment

Chapter 36 Review

In Chapter 36, your child studied the identification of letters and grouping by numbers.

Your child learned:
- Recognition of sight words.
- Recognition of letters G through L.
- Comprehension of number words.

To review what your child has learned, do the activities below. Review the pages of this chapter with your child if he or she is having difficulty in any of the following areas. You can also review and reinforce the skills in this section with the additional activities listed below.

1. Have your child place the letter i on the lines and read the word.

___ t   ___s   ___f   ___n

2. Ask your child to draw a line from the number to the number word that matches.

1	four
2	three
3	two
4	one
5	five

3. Tell your child to match the beginning sounds with the number words.

S	9
T	5
F	2
N	6

Additional Activities

Here are some simple and fun things you can do with your child to practice what you have worked on in this chapter. To help reinforce what was learned in this chapter, try these activities.

1. Make letter cards A-Z and have your child place cards on objects around the house that begin with those sounds.
2. Make number word cards and have your child match the number word to a number in the house.
3. Chant "Five Little Monkeys" and have your child hold up the correct number word that corresponds with the spoken number.

Chapter 37

Today's lesson will be lots of fun as we join Paige and Marco while they watch Sam play games at the carnival!

While Sam tests his strength, you will have a good time learning how to:
- Recognize letters
- Use American Sign Language
- Recognize Number words

Now let's see what's going on at the carnival!

Animal Book

Keep working on your animal book. Draw a picture of an animal that begins with M, N, O, P, Q, and R. Once you have drawn the picture and written the animal's name in the space at the boxes bottom, have an adult help you cut the boxes out of the page and add them to your book.

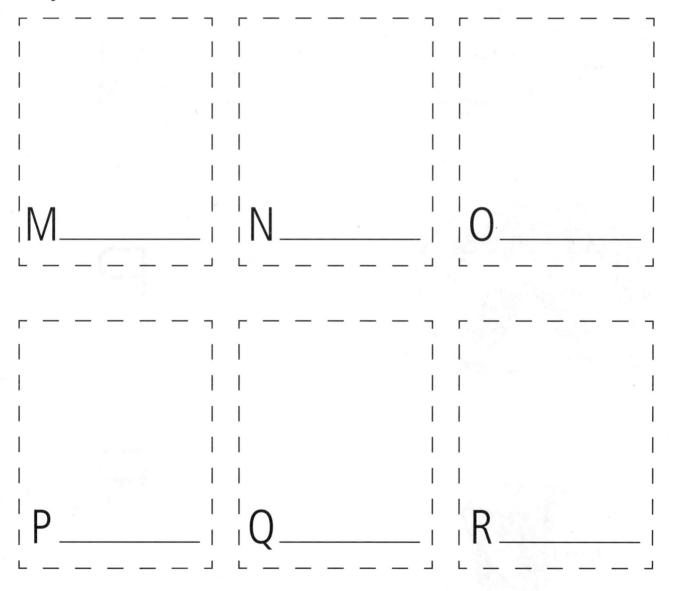

M_____   N_____   O_____

P_____   Q_____   R_____

Beginning Sounds

Draw a line from the letter to the group of items that correspond with the beginning sound.

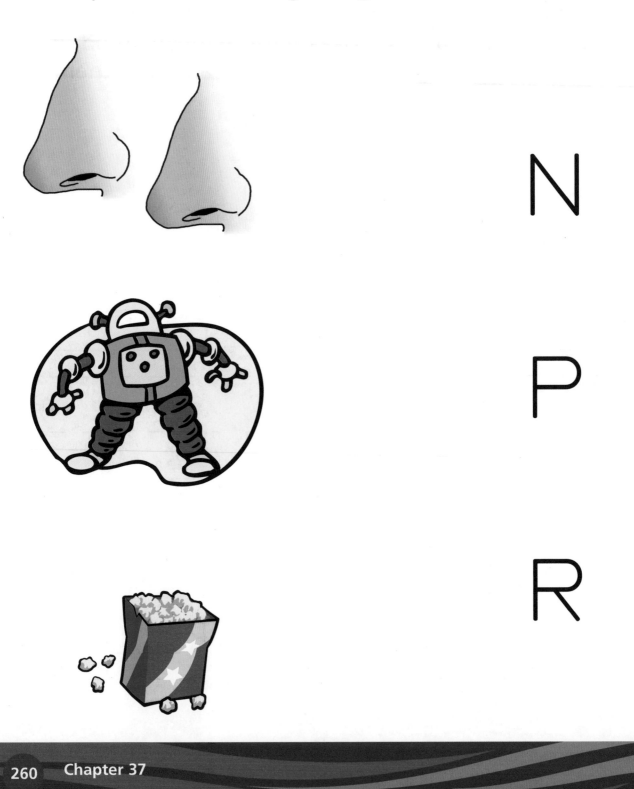

N

P

R

Sign Language

Using the pictures below, sign the corresponding sight words. Practice writing the words and signing them.

I

and

the

Number Words

Complete the sentences below by filling in the missing number words.

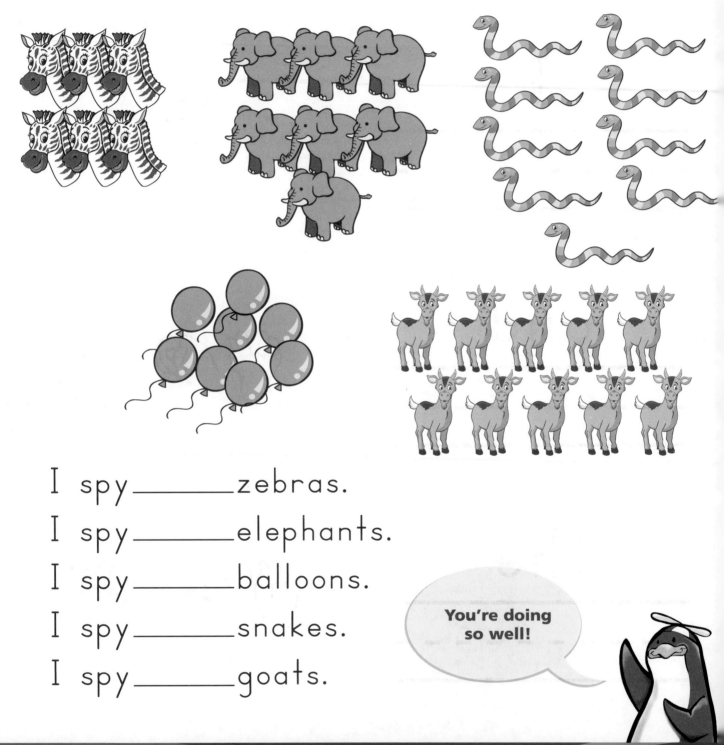

I spy _____ zebras.

I spy _____ elephants.

I spy _____ balloons.

I spy _____ snakes.

I spy _____ goats.

You're doing so well!

Number Words

Complete the sentences below by filling in the missing number words.

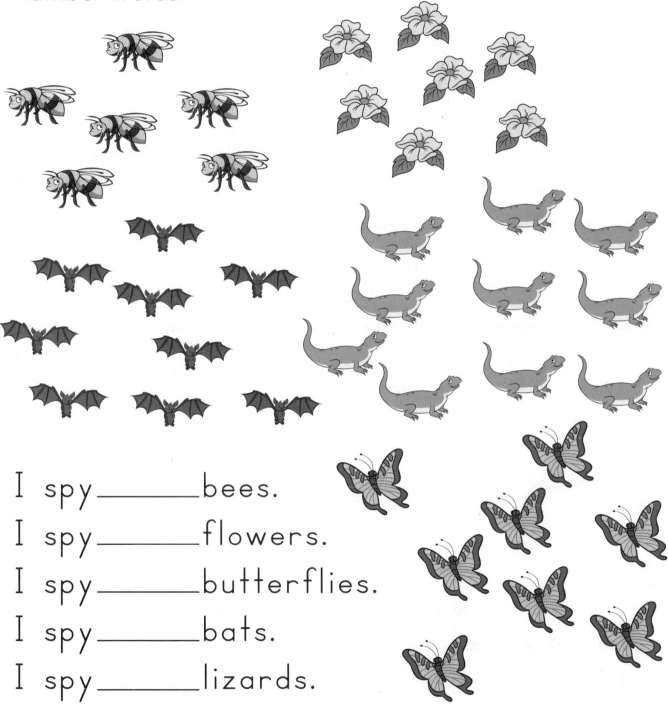

I spy_____bees.
I spy_____flowers.
I spy_____butterflies.
I spy_____bats.
I spy_____lizards.

Assessment

Chapter 37 Review

In Chapter 37, your child studied recognition of letters and grouping by numbers.

Your child learned:
- Recognition of sight words.
- American Sign Language (ASL) for sight words (I, the, and).
- Recognition of letters M through R.
- Comprehension of number words.

To review what your child has learned, do the activities below. Review the pages of this chapter with your child if he or she is having difficulty in any of the following areas. You can also review and reinforce the skills in this section with the additional activities listed below.

1. Have your child put these words in alphabetical order:

parrot   quack

not   octopus

2. Ask your child to make words by placing the provided letters on the correct line.

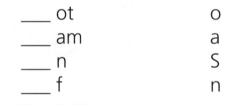

___ ot   o

___ am   a

___ n   S

___ f   n

3. Write number words next to the number.

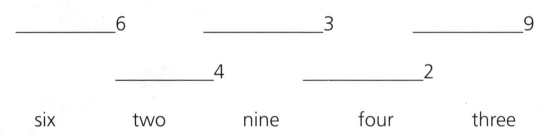

_____6   _____3   _____9

_____4   _____2

six   two   nine   four   three

Additional Activities

Here are some simple and fun things you can do with your child to practice what you have worked on in this chapter. To help reinforce what was learned in this chapter, try these activities.

1. Point to objects around the house and have your child say the beginning sounds.
2. Randomly place six objects on a table that begin with the letters A, B, C, D, E, and F. Then have your child place the objects in alphabetical order.

Chapter 38

Today's lesson will be lots of fun as we join Bogart while he sleds down a hill of snow!

While he explores, you will have a good time learning:
- Letter review
- American Sign Language
- Sight words in sentences
- Numerical order

Now let's see what's happening in the snow!

Animal Book

Draw a picture of an animal that begins with S, T, U, V, W, and X: Y and Z are on the next page. Add these pictures to your Animal Book.

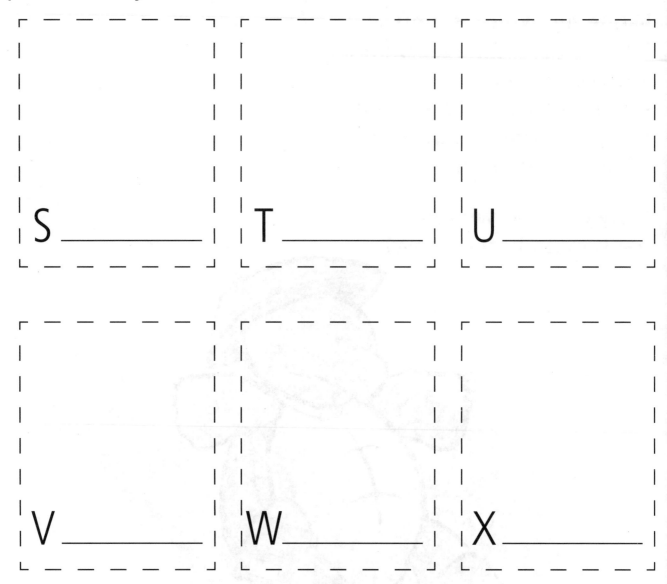

S_____   T_____   U_____

V_____   W_____   X_____

Animal Book

Now that you have completed your pictures, have an adult help you cut along the dotted lines and put your animal book in order beginning with A and ending in Z. Read your first book to a friend.

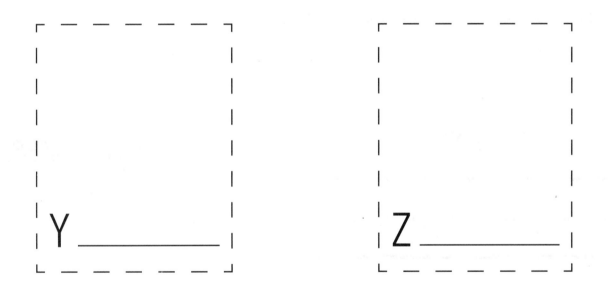

Sign Language

Using the pictures below, sign the sight words below. Practice writing the words below and signing them.

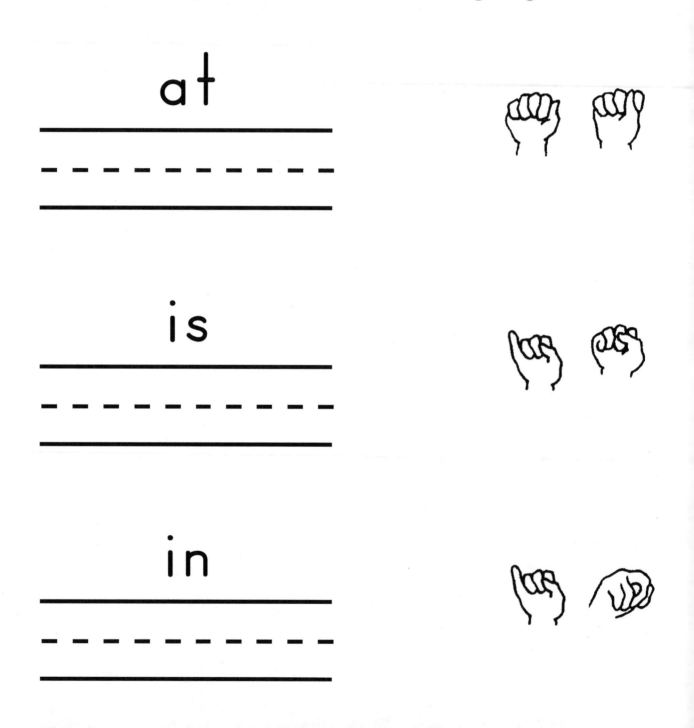

at

is

in

Completing Sentences

Place the missing sight words in the sentences. Read the sentences aloud.

The doll is_____the toy box.

The cat_____in the tree.

The girl is_____ the bus stop.

at   is   in

Great job!

Number Sequencing

Place these numbers in order.

You're on a roll!

21   25   22

23   24   20

_____   _____   _____

_____   _____   _____

Number Sequencing

Fill in the missing numbers in order.

20 _____ 22 _____ 24

25

Great job!

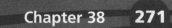

Assessment

Chapter 38 Review

In Chapter 38, your child studied recognition of letters and grouping by numbers.

Your child learned:
- Recognition of letters S through Z.
- American Sign Language (ASL) for sight words (at, is, in).
- Comprehension of sight words in sentences.
- Number order.

To review what your child has learned, do the activities below. Review the pages of this chapter with your child if he or she is having difficulty in any of the following areas. You can also review and reinforce the skills in this section with the additional activities listed below.

1. Have your child place these numbers in order:

17	3	20	11	2	13	12	8
1	6	14	16	10	5	19	7
4	9	18	15				

2. Tell your child to make words by filling in the middle "a" sound in each word.

f___t   c___t
m___t   s___t

3. Direct your child to fill in the missing numbers.

15	16	___	___	19	___	21
22	___	24	___	___	___	28
29	30					

Additional Activities

Here are some simple and fun things you can do with your child to practice what you have worked on in this chapter. To help reinforce what was learned in this chapter, try these activities.

1. Have your child find the numbers 15 through 20 in and around your home.
2. Help your child sign his or her name. Try signing the names of the members of your family.
3. In addition to those in activity #2 above, can your child think of any other "–at" words? Ask your child to make up a silly "–at" rhyme.

Chapter 39

Today's lesson will be lots of fun as we join Paige and Sam as they play with a ball on the beach!

While they explore, you will have a good time learning:
• Name recognition
• Money concepts

Now let's see what's happening at the beach!

Your Name and Mine

Write your name on the line below. Circle the letters that your name has in common with Quincy and Sam.

So, do they match?

Quincy

Sam

That's it!

Letter Name Scavenger Hunt

Write your name in squares on the top line. Find items that begin with each letter of your name and draw them in the squares below each letter.

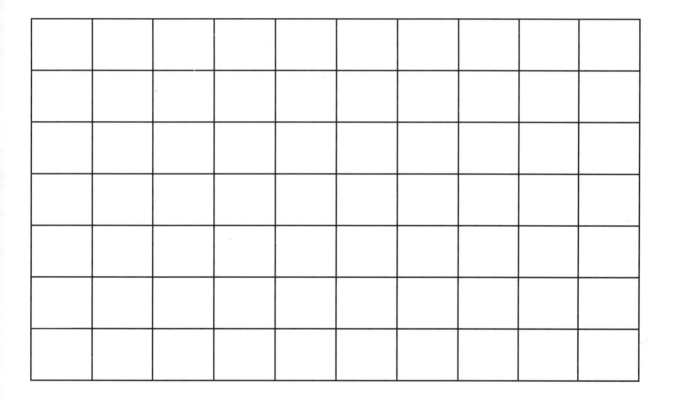

This looks fun!

Your Name and Mine

Write the value below each letter of your name and add up the sum.

Each consonant is worth 1 cent.
Each vowel is worth 5 cents.

For Example:

J   O   D   I

1 + 5 + 1 + 5 = 12

You try:

_____ _____ _____ _____ _____

_____ _____ _____ _____ _____

Money

You have 50 cents in your pocket. You cannot spend any more than 50 cents. Circle the items below that you are able to buy.

52
cents

66
cents

10
cents

25
cents

Coins

Draw a line from each coin to the amount that it is worth.

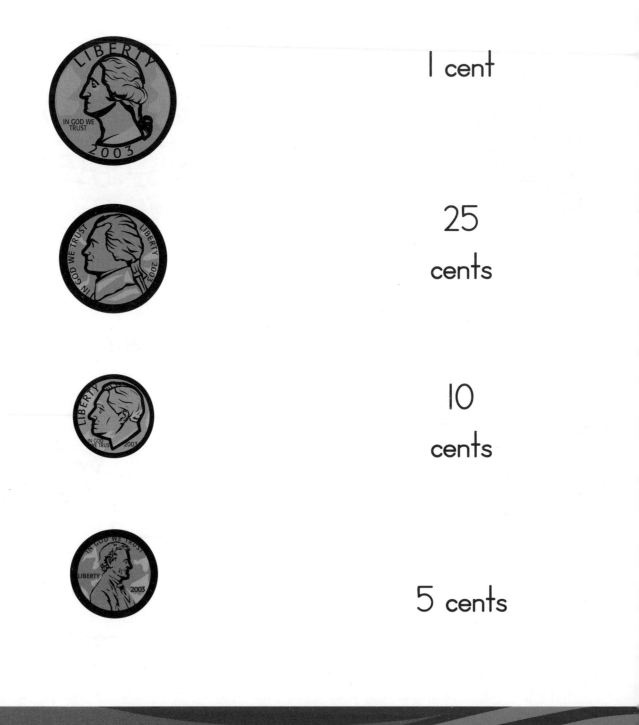

1 cent

25 cents

10 cents

5 cents

Assessment

Chapter 39 Review

In this chapter, your child studied letter recognition, beginning sounds, and coins.

Your child learned:
- Letter identification.
- Recognition of consonants and vowels.
- Recognition of coins and their values.
- Numeric value.

The following activities will allow your child to review the things studied in this chapter. If your child is having difficulty in any of the areas below, review the pages of this chapter with your child. You can also review and reinforce the skills covered in this chapter with the additional activities at the bottom of this page.

1. Have your child circle the letters that her or his name has in common with:

F r a n c e s   J o n a t h a n

2. Help your child draw a picture of an item that begins with each letter in her or his name.

3. Ask your child to determine the value of her or his name using these rules:

- Each consonant is worth 1 cent.
- Each vowel is worth 10 cents.

Additional Activities
Below are some interactive ways you and your child can practice what you have worked on in this chapter. These activities will reinforce the skills your child studied on the previous pages.

1. The next time you go to the store with your child, give him or her $.50 to buy something.
2. When reading a favorite book, ask your child to show you the vowels.
3. Empty the coins from your wallet or purse and ask your child to name them and tell you their value.

Chapter 40

Today's lesson will be lots of fun as we join Marco and Paige while they fly high in the clouds!

While they explore, you will have a good time learning:
- Word families
- Name recognition

Now let's see what's going on amidst the clouds!

Word Families: -at

Unscramble the letters to form words in the -at word family.

atb   tac   ast

atf   tam   aht

I know you can do this!

Word Families: -it

Unscramble the letters to form words in the -it word family.

itf   thi   pti

its

This is a breeze for you!

Same Names

Write your name above the first circle below. Place the letters that are the same in your name and Christina's name in the middle. Place the letters that are different in the circles under each person's name.

_____ Christina

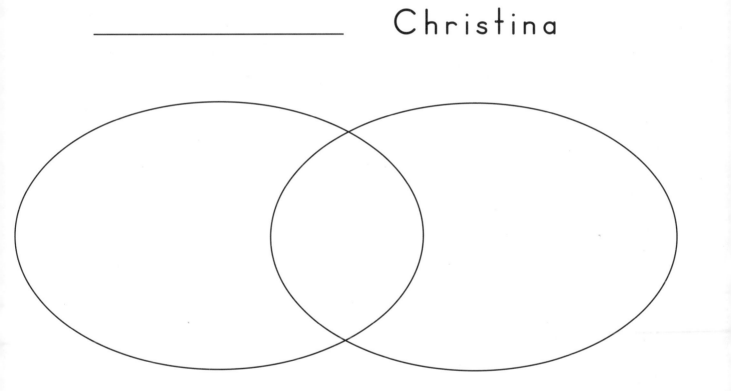

Same Letters

How many letters do these names have that are the same?

JOE   SAM

JOHN   MATT

Number of Js   _____

Number of Os   _____

Number of Es   _____

Number of Hs   _____

Number of Ns   _____

Number of Ss   _____

Number of As   _____

Number of Ms   _____

Number of Ts   _____

Which name has the most Ts? _____

Numbers I Know

Complete the following number information about yourself.

I am _____ years old.

My address is _____

_____ .

My phone number is _____ .

My birthday is _____ .

I have _____ family members in my house.

I have _____ pets.

It's good to know this information.

Assessment

Chapter 40 Review

In Chapter 40, your child studied word families, letter comparisons, and how to answer questions.

Your child learned:
- Recognition of rhyming words.
- Identification of same letters between two words.
- Comprehension of "most."

Work with your child on the chapter review activities shown below. If your child has difficulty with any of these exercises, go back through the chapter with him or her to review the material. You can also review and reinforce these skills with your child using the exercises in the additional activities section below.

1. Ask your child to unscramble these words:

   "at" word family: tab   cta   tah

   "it" word family: hti   tis   ibt

2. Using your name and your child's name, follow the directions for the "Same Names" activity on page 283.

3. Ask your child: How many letters do these names have that are the same?

                    Sam   Mark   Mary

   Number of *s*s _____
   Number of *a*s _____
   Number of *m*s _____
   Number of *r*s _____
   Number of *k*s _____
   Number of *y*s _____

   Which letter appears most often?

Additional Activities
Here are some interactive ways you and your child can practice what you have worked on in this chapter. These activities will reinforce the skills your child studied on the previous pages.

1. Help your child make a card with emergency numbers on it that your child can keep in his or her backpack. You can use an index card for the numbers and take it to a local copy shop to have it laminated.
2. Play a rhyming game with your child using "at" and "it." Your child can write the words as she or he thinks of them.

Chapter 41

Today's lesson will be lots of fun as we join Bogart and Marco while they swim in the pool.

While they splash, you will have a good time learning:
• Word families
• Ordinal numbers

Now let's see what's happening at the pool!

Word Families -am

Unscramble the letters to form words in the -am word family.

a m h   j m a   a m P

S m a

I'm in one of these!

Word Families -in

Unscramble the letters to form words in the -in word family.

nfi   npi   tni

nwi

You're the best!

Ordinal Numbers

Put the numbers in order.

Second   1

Fifth   2

Fourth   3

Third   4

First   5

Ordinal Numbers

Place an X on the first child in line, circle the third child in line, and put a box around the fifth child in line.

Good Job!

Ordinal Numbers

Color the first elephant yellow, second elephant green, third elephant gray, fourth elephant blue, and fifth elephant red.

Assessment

Chapter 41 Review

Your child studied word families and numerical order in Chapter 41.

Your child learned:
- Recognition of rhyming words using word families "-am" and "-in."
- Comprehension of ordinal numbers.

The following activities will provide a review of what your child has learned. If he or she has any difficulty in any of the areas below, go back through the pages of this chapter with your child. You can also review and reinforce the skills in this section with the additional activities listed below.

1. Ask your child to unscramble the letters to form words in the:

"-am" word family: Pma   mah   maj

"-in" word family: niw   pni   nif

2. Have your child put the number next to the word it represents.

    Fourth ___   Second ___   First ___   Third ___   Fifth ___

3. Explain to your child that these animals are in a line from left to right. Have her or him circle the first animal in line, place an "x" on the third animal in line, and put a box around the fifth animal in line.

Additional Activities

Here are some simple and fun things you can do with your child to practice what you have worked on in this chapter. To help reinforce what was learned in this chapter, try these activities.

1. When reading a favorite book, ask your child to identify all of the words that are in the "-am" and "-in" word families.
2. Have your child put five favorite stuffed animals in a line. Ask him or her to point to the fifth animal, the second animal, and the fourth animal. You can repeat this game by changing the order of the animals.
3. Next time you wait in a line with your child, ask him or her what place you are in line.

Chapter 42

Today's lesson will be lots of fun as we join Bogart and Sam as they zoom around the sky in an airplane.

While they explore, you will have a good time learning about:
• Family trees
• Number orders

Now let's see what's happening in the clouds!

Family Tree

Draw a line from the picture of the family member to their correct place.

Grandparents

Parents

Children

Family Tree

Using the lines below, create your own family tree. Place the names of your grandparents on the bottom line, your parents on the middle lines, and you and your siblings on the top lines. Add more lines if you need to.

_____
(brother or sister)

_____
(brother or sister)

_____
(brother or sister)

_____
(brother or sister)

_____
(mother)

_____
(father)

_____
(grandmother)

_____
(grandfather)

_____
(grandmother)

_____
(grandfather)

Word Families -an

Unscramble the letters to form words in the -an word family.

anc   fna   nma

npa   tna   nav

This is a breeze for you!

Missing Numbers

Fill in the missing numbers.

80   _____   _____   83

84   85   _____   87

88   _____

You did it!

Number Order

Place these numbers in order.

11   15   13   12   14   16

___ ___ ___ ___ ___ ___

26   28   30   25   27   29

___ ___ ___ ___ ___ ___

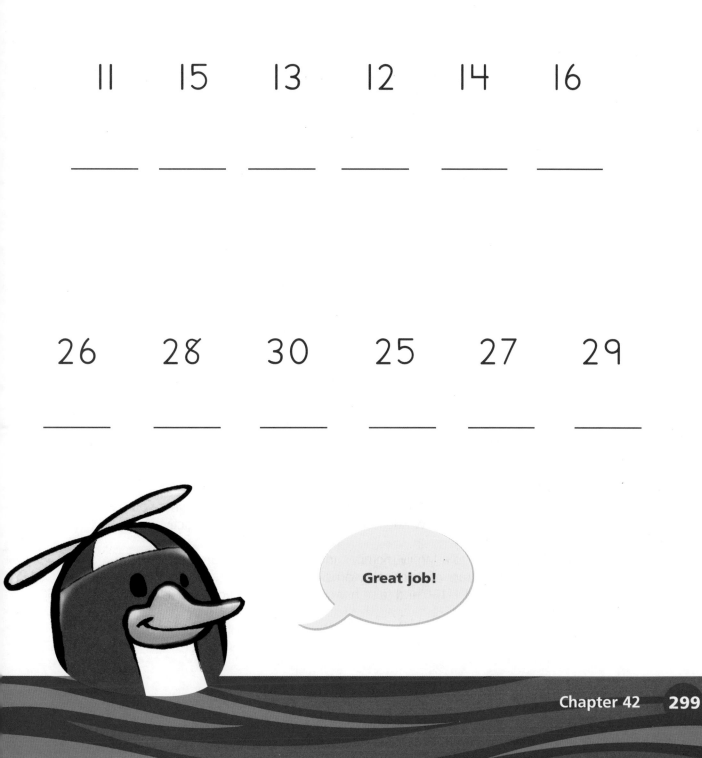

Great job!

Assessment

Chapter 42 Review

In Chapter 42, your child studied number order, basic concepts of family trees, and word families.

Your child learned:
- Basic genealogy (family relationships).
- Numeric order.
- Recognition of rhyming words using word family "-an."

To review what your child has learned, do the activities below. Review the pages of this chapter with your child if he or she is having difficulty in any of the following areas. You can also review and reinforce the skills in this section with the additional activities listed below.

1. Instruct your child to write the number that will come before the given numbers.

    __9   __18   __23   __44   __61

2. Have your child draw a line to the correct family word.

    cat   -an
    fan
    tan
    fat
    pan   -at
    sat

3. Tell your child to write the number that will come after the given number.

    10__   24__   57__   86__

Additional Activities

Here are some simple and fun things you can do with your child to practice what you have worked on in this chapter. To help reinforce what was learned in this chapter, try these activities.

1. Have your child write a note to a family member. Include an illustration too.
2. Ask your child to draw a picture of three -an words.
3. Tell your child to count aloud 1-100 and raise her or his hand at all of the 10s (10, 20, 30, 40, 50, 60, 70, 80, 90, and 100).

Chapter 43

Today's lesson will be lots of fun as we join Bogart and Marco while they play at the carnival.

As they play, you will have a good time learning:
• Word families
• Ordinal numbers

Now let's see what's happening at the carnival!

Poetry

Read the poem below. Circle the rhyming words and underline the color words.

Yellow

Green is go,
And red is stop,
And yellow is peaches
With cream on top.

Earth is brown,
And blue is sky,
Yellow looks well
On a butterfly.

Clouds are white,
Black, pink or mocha,
Yellow is a dish of
Tapioca.

Sequencing

Place these numbers in order:

51   56   58   60   50   52

53   55   57   54   59

___ ___ ___ ___ ___ ___

___ ___ ___ ___ ___

This is fun!

What Number am I?

I have curves.
I do not have
straight lines.
I am more than two.
I am less than four.

What number am I?

This is cool!

What Number am I?

I have lines and curves.
I look like a backwards "P."
I am more than eight.
I am less than ten.

What number am I?

You got it daddy-o!

What Number am I?

I have lines and curves.
I am two numbers.
I am more than fourteen.
I am less than sixteen.

What number am I?

You're a
cool cat!

Assessment

Chapter 43 Review

In Chapter 43, your child studied recognition of letters, rhyming words, color words, and grouping by numbers.

Your child learned:
- Basic concepts of poetry.
- Number identification.
- Number sequencing.

To review what your child has learned, do the activities below. Review the pages of this chapter with your child if he or she is having difficulty in any of the following areas. You can also review and reinforce the skills in this section with the additional activities listed below.

1. Have your child draw a line to the word and picture that rhyme.

dog   cat   coat   blue

2. Ask your child to draw a picture of a word that rhymes with:

cat   go   red   top

3. Ask your child to guess the two numbers below.

I am straight.   I am almost 100.
There are two of me.   There are two of me.
I am bigger than 10.   I am bigger than 98.
I am smaller than 12.   I am smaller than 100.
What number am I?   What number am I?

Additional Activities

Here are some simple and fun things you can do with your child to practice what you have worked on in this chapter. To help reinforce what was learned in this chapter, try these activities.

1. Ask your child to think of five groups of words that rhyme.
2. Have your child count aloud from 1-50 and raise her or his hand at all of the 5s (5, 10, 15, 20, 25, 30, 35, 40, 45, and 50).
3. See if your child can think up a "guess a number" riddle.

Chapter 44

Today's lesson will be lots of fun as we join Quincy and Sam while they play in the garden.

While they explore, you will have a good time learning:
- Poetry
- Sequencing

Now let's see what's happening in the garden!

Poetry

Read the poem below. Circle the rhyming words and underline the number words.

One, Two, Buckle My Shoe

One, two, buckle my shoe.

Three, four, knock at the door.

Five, six, pick up sticks.

Seven, eight, lay them straight.

Nine, ten, a big, fat hen.

You are groovin'!

Poetry

Create a rhyming poem. You can either tell your favorite to an adult or make up your own and have an adult write it down. Make sure there are rhyming words in it.

_____

_____

_____

_____

_____

_____

_____

_____

_____

_____

_____

Missing Picture

Look at the patterns below. Draw the missing pictures.

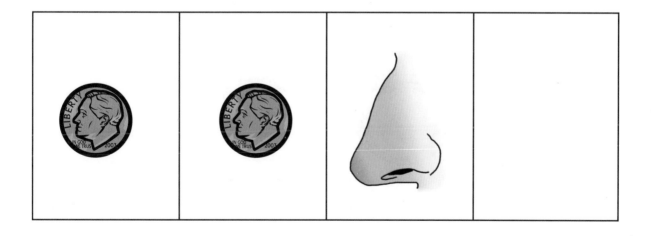

Missing Picture

Look at the patterns below. Draw the missing pictures.

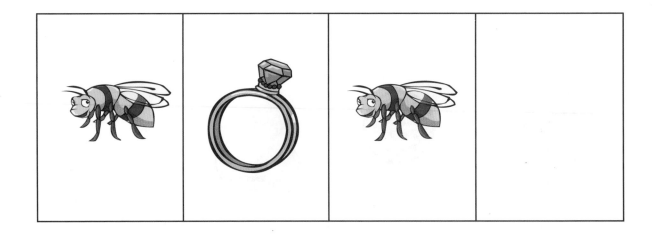

Missing Picture

Look at the patterns below. Draw the missing pictures.

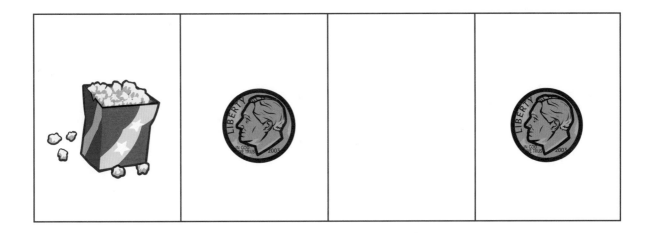

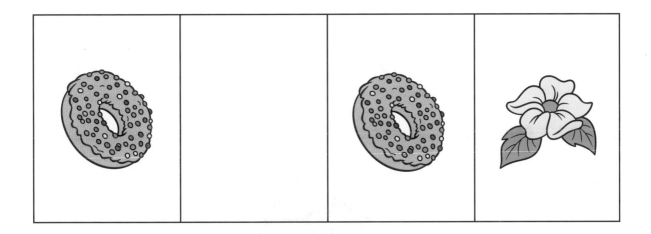

Number Order

Place these numbers in order.

6   5   9   7   8   4

___ ___ ___ ___ ___ ___

13   14   15   12   16   11

___ ___ ___ ___ ___ ___

Great job!

Assessment

Chapter 44 Review

In Chapter 44, your child studied recognition of letters, rhyming words, and how to group by numbers. In this chapter, some activities were repeated to reinforce your child's learning.

Your child learned:
- Basic concepts of poetry.
- Visual discernment of sequences and missing pictures.

To review what your child has learned, do the activities below. Review the pages of this chapter with your child if he or she is having difficulty in any of the following areas. You can also review and reinforce the skills in this section with the additional activities listed below.

1. Have your child sound out words that rhyme with:

   it_____   at_____   is_____   in_____

2. Tell your child to draw a line between the rhyming words.

cat	fun
top	stop
run	bed
red	fat

3. Have your child fill in the missing items with the pattern.

■	X	■	X	

#	#	I		#

	4	2	4	2	4		

Additional Activities

Here are some simple and fun things you can do with your child to practice what you have worked on in this chapter. To help reinforce what was learned in this chapter, try these activities.

1. Have your child use coins to make a pattern.
2. Using the coin pattern your child created, have your child close his or her eyes as you take away a coin. Have your child identify the missing coin in the pattern. You can trade roles and play this game again.
3. Ask your child to sing a favorite song and identify rhyming words.

Chapter 45

Today's lesson will be lots of fun as we join Quincy and Rosa as they study penguins at the South Pole.

While they explore, you will have a good time learning how to:
- Form words
- Count by 2s

Now let's see what's happening on the ice!

Making Words

Using the "-at" word family, fill in the letters below to make words. Read the words aloud.

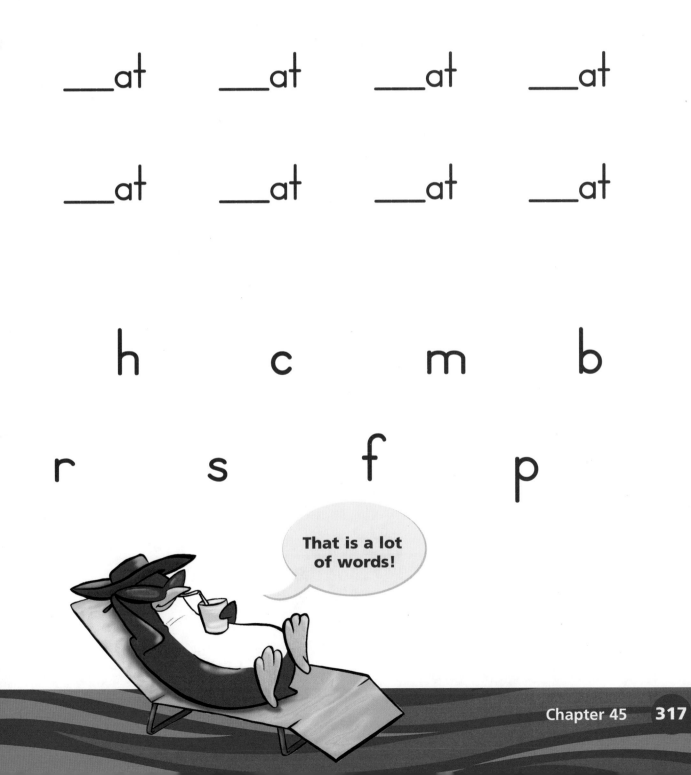

__at   __at   __at   __at

__at   __at   __at   __at

h   c   m   b

r   s   f   p

That is a lot of words!

Illustrating Words-

Draw pictures of the "-at" family words from the previous page.

You are good at drawing!

Illustrating Words

When counting by 2s you only say the even numbers out loud. You would count by saying "2, 4, 6, 8, 10, 12, 14, 16, 18, 20," and so on. You try it.

Complete the dot-to-dot picture by connecting the even numbers together.

Counting by 2s

This is how we count by 2s:
2, 4, 6, 8, 10, 12, 14, 16, 18, 20.

Circle the clouds as you count by 2s from 0 to 20.
There are some clouds that don't belong.

0...2...4...6 ...8...10!

Number Sequencing

Place these numbers in order.

Write on the lines below!

34

35

39

31

32

30

38

37

36

33

___ ___ ___ ___ ___ ___

___ ___ ___ ___ ___

Good work!

Assessment

Chapter 45 Review

In Chapter 45, your child studied the identification of word families, the illustration of words, and how to count and order numbers.

Your child learned:
- Recognition of words using the word family "-at."
- Depiction of words with illustration.
- How to count by 2s.
- Number sequencing.

To review what your child has learned, do the activities below. Review the pages of this chapter with your child if he or she is having difficulty in any of the following areas. You can also review and reinforce the skills in this section with the additional activities listed below.

1. Have your child fill in the missing even numbers.

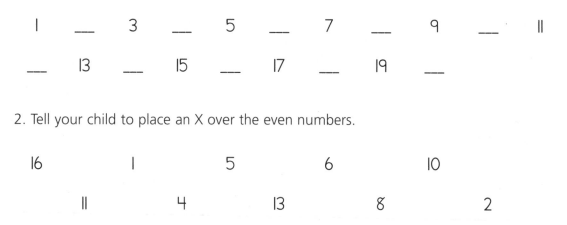

1 __ 3 __ 5 __ 7 __ 9 __ 11

__ 13 __ 15 __ 17 __ 19 __

2. Tell your child to place an X over the even numbers.

16   1   5   6   10

11   4   13   8   2

3. Ask your child to write five -at words.

Additional Activities

Here are some simple and fun things you can do with your child to practice what you have worked on in this chapter. To help reinforce what was learned in this chapter, try these activities.

1. Have your child do the following: count from 1 to 20 aloud and raise your hand when saying the even numbers (2, 4, 6, 8, 10, 12, 14, 16, 18, and 20).
2. On a car trip, ask your child to point out even numbers.
3. With your child, make up a poem or song using six -at words.

Chapter 46

Today's lesson will be lots of fun as we join Paige and Rosa while they pick carrots in the garden.

While they work, you will have a good time learning:
- Word formation
- Shape identification
- Numerical order

Making Words

Add the letter "i" to the beginning of each word.
Sound it out on your own.

__t

__s

__n

__f

I like letters!

Making Words

Add the letter "a" to the beginning of each word.
Sound it out on your own.

__t

__s

__n   __m

Awesome!

Identifying Shapes

Identify which shape has the amount of sides given.

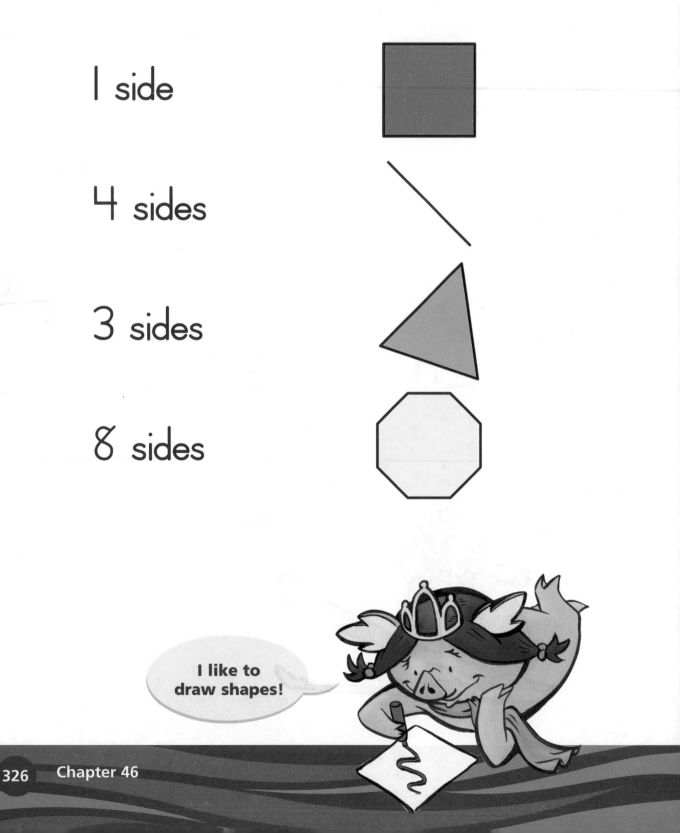

1 side

4 sides

3 sides

8 sides

I like to draw shapes!

Number Sequencing

Place these numbers in order.

Number Sequencing

Match the number of wheels to the
pictures to form a graph.

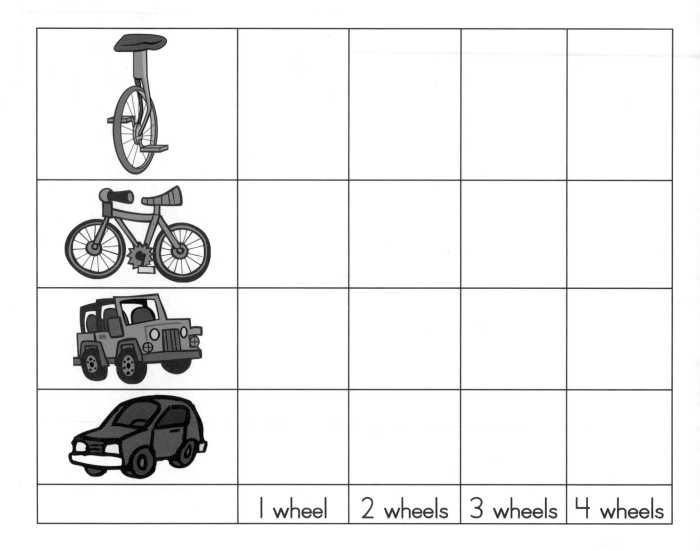

	1 wheel	2 wheels	3 wheels	4 wheels

I love to
graph!

Assessment

Chapter 46 Review

In Chapter 46, your child studied word formation, shape recognition, number order, and graph use.

Your child learned how to:
- Form words using the letter "i".
- Form words using the letter "a".
- Identify shapes
- Sequence Numbers
- Graph

The following activities will allow your child to review the things studied in this chapter. If your child is having difficulty in any of the areas below, review the pages of this chapter with your child. You can also review and reinforce the skills covered in this chapter with the additional activities at the bottom of this page.

1. Tell your child to look at the graph below and decide which shape has the most and which has the least.

5				
4				
3				
2				
1				
	Triangle	Circle	Heart	Diamond

2. Have your child place the following letters on the correct line to make a word. Then ask him or her to sound out the new word.

    ___in   ___in   ___in   f   t   w

                                                               s   b   f

    ___it   ___it   ___it

Additional Activities

Here is an interactive way you and your child can practice what you have worked on in this chapter. This activity will reinforce the skills your child studied on previous pages.

1. Tell your child to write a sentence using these words.
   (Hint: *I* is the first word and *kid* is the last word.)

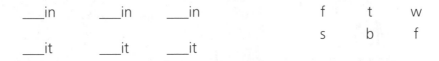

            am   I   kid   a   good

Chapter 47

Today's lesson will be lots of fun as we join Sam as he helps out on the farm by driving a tractor.

While he works, you will have a good time learning:
• Opposites
• Identification
• Numerical order

Now let's see what's going on down on the farm!

Opposites

Draw a line from each item to its opposite.

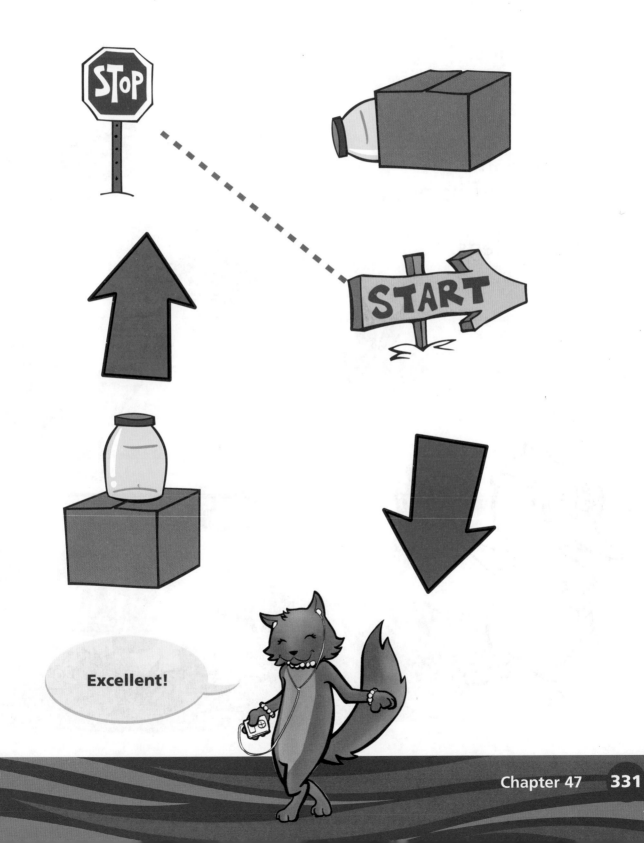

Which one?

Quincy is using his bug net to catch bugs.
Which bug did he catch?

It has wings.

It has many colors.

It is the same on
each side of its body.

It has no legs.

Which One?

Rosa is visiting the pet store to get a new pet. Which pet did she choose?

It has four legs.

It has two eyes on the sides of its head.

It does not shed fur.

It is green.

I think that I'd make the best pet of all!

Number Sequencing

Place these numbers in order.

Which Season?

Look at the pictures below and decide if the clothing is what you would wear in winter or summer. Graph the information.

	Winter clothing	Summer clothing

Sometimes I can't decide what to wear!

Assessment

Chapter 47 Review

Your child studied the identification of opposites, problem solving, number order, and graph use in Chapter 47.

Your child learned how to:
- Recognize opposites.
- Deduce using reason.
- Sequence numbers.
- Graph.

To review what your child has learned, do the activities below. Review the pages of this chapter with your child if he or she is having difficulty in any of the following areas. You can also review and reinforce the skills in this section with the additional activities listed below.

1. Using these clues, have your child decide which animal is being described.

> I have black spots on me.
> I am an insect.
> I sometimes fly.
> I have a red shell.
> What am I?

2. On a separate piece of paper have your child make a graph of the following apples:

Additional Activities

Here are some simple and fun things you can do with your child to practice what you have worked on in this chapter. To help reinforce what was learned in this chapter, try these activities.

1. Help your child think of three new opposite pairs. Have your child draw a picture of these things and explain to you why they are opposites.
2. Tell your child to look at the graph in activity 2 above and identify the most apples and the least apples. Think of some items from your child's room that he or she can graph in this way.
3. Using this riddle, enjoy the fruit described with your child.

> I am usually red, yellow, or green.
> I am round.
> If you cut me in the middle, you will find a star.
> What am I?

Chapter 48

Today's lesson will be lots of fun as we join Marco as he slides down a hill of snow on his belly!

While he races, you will have a good time learning how to:
• Match
• Sequence numerically
• Count by 10s

Now let's see what's happening in the snow!

Matching Cards

Fill in the boxes below with one letter in each box.
Use the letters A, B, C, D, E, and F.

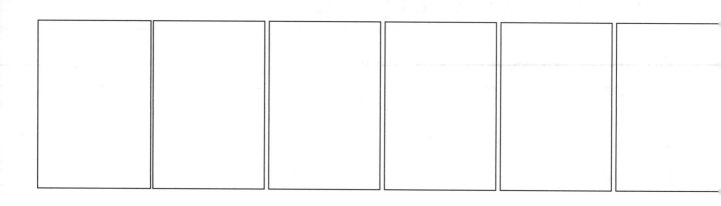

Find food labels or magazine pictures of words that
begin with each letter. Glue those pictures to the
boxes below.

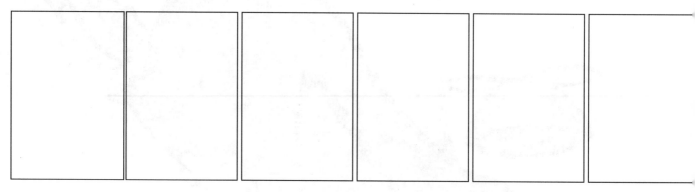

Cut out all 12 boxes and enjoy a matching game.

I like to
play cards!

Matching Cards

Fill in the boxes below with one letter in each box.
Use the letters G, H, I, J, K, and L.

Find food labels or magazine pictures of words that begin with each letter. Glue those pictures to the boxes below.

Cut out all 12 boxes and enjoy a matching game.

This sounds like lots of fun!

Number Sequencing

Place these numbers in order.

Counting by 10s

When counting by 10s you only say the numbers that end in 0 out loud. You would count by saying, "10, 20, 30, 40, 50, 60, 70, 80, 90, and 100." You try it.

Complete the dot-to-dot picture by connecting the 10s together.

Great job!

Counting by 10s

Count out loud by 10s to 50: "10, 20, 30, 40, and 50."

Now color the cows below in order as you count by 10s.

Assessment

Chapter 48 Review

In Chapter 48, your child studied how to recognize letters, place numbers in sequence, and group by numbers.

Your child learned:
- Phonics review (A-F).
- Phonics review (G-L).
- Number sequencing.
- How to count by 10s.

To review what your child has learned, do the activities below. Review the pages of this chapter with your child if he or she is having difficulty in any of the following areas. You can also review and reinforce the skills in this section with the additional activities listed below.

1. Ask your child to place these letters in alphabetical order:

    D   J   A   N   G   L

    ___   ___   ___   ___   ___   ___

Additional Activities

Here are some simple and fun things you can do with your child to practice what you have worked on in this chapter. To help reinforce what was learned in this chapter, try these activities.

1. Get 10 dimes and have your child count them by 10s. Ask your child to tell you other ways to describe 10 dimes (100 cents, 1 dollar). Direct your child to write only the number 10s counting from 1-100.

   —   —   —   —   —   —   —   —   —   —

2. Ask your child to think of a word that goes with each letter of the alphabet.
3. Help your child practice writing words. Read the following words aloud as your child writes them on a piece of paper. These words will help your child be a great reader!

go, this, look, like, it, in, I, am, is, if, here, there, can, are

Chapter 49

Today's lesson will be lots of fun as we join Quincy and Sam while they visit their friends at the zoo!

While they explore, you will have a good time reviewing how to:
• Match
• Sequence numerically
• Count by 10s

Now let's see what's going on at the zoo!

Matching Cards

Fill in the boxes below with one letter in each box.
Use the letters M, N, O, P, Q, and R.

Find food labels or magazine pictures of words that
begin with each letter. Glue those pictures to the
boxes below.

Cut out all 12 boxes and enjoy a matching game.

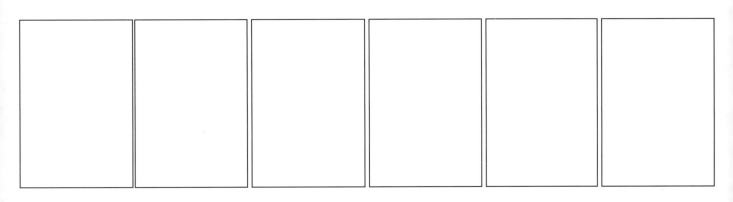

**Rosa starts
with R!**

Matching Cards

Fill in the boxes below with one letter in each box.
Use the letters S, T, U, V, W, and X.

Find food labels or magazine pictures of words that begin with each letter. Glue those pictures to the boxes below.

Cut out all 12 boxes and enjoy a matching game.

I wonder
what will start
with W?

Number Sequencing

Place these numbers in order.

You can count very high!

66

69

68

60

61

65

63

64

62

67

_ _ _ _ _ _ _ _ _ _

_ _ _ _ _ _ _ _ _ _

Write on these lines!

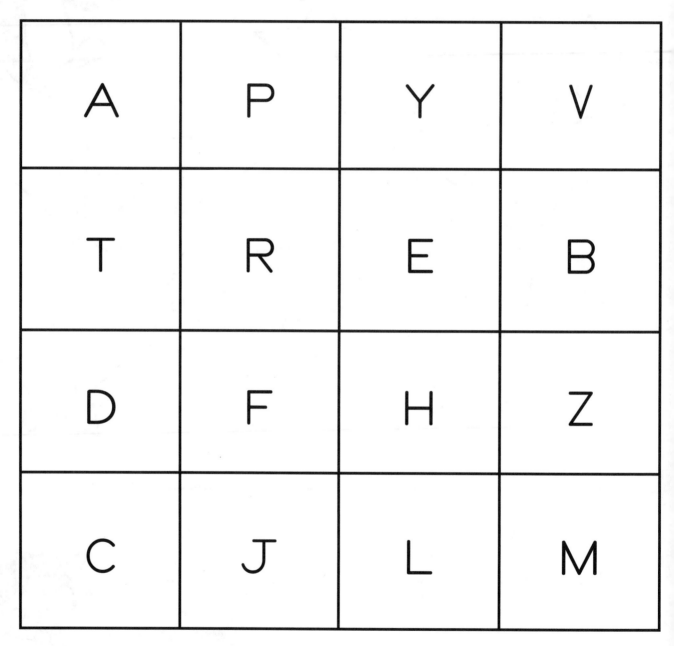

Letter Bingo

Using the board below, play bingo. On the opposite page, cut out the cards and use the beginning sound of each picture to identify which letter to cover.

A	P	Y	V
T	R	E	B
D	F	H	Z
C	J	L	M

Assessment

Chapter 49 Review

In this chapter, your child studied how to recognize letters, place numbers in sequence, and group by numbers.

Your child learned:
- Phonics review (M-R).
- Phonics review (S-X).
- Number sequencing (60-69).
- How to count by 10s.

Do the following activities to review what your child has learned. If your child is having difficulty in any of the areas below, go back through the pages of this chapter with your child. You can also review and reinforce the skills in this section with the additional activities listed below.

1. Tell your child to place these letters in alphabetical order:

G   S   B   V   P   L   Z

___   ___   ___   ___   ___   ___   ___

2. Have your child place these numbers in numerical order.

11   29   1   20   34   6   43   16   50

___   ___   ___   ___   ___   ___   ___   ___   ___

3. Ask your child to put these words in alphabetical order:

stop   cat   fin   top   van

_____   _____   _____   _____   _____

Additional Activities

Below are some interactive ways you and your child can review what you have worked on in this chapter. These activities will reinforce the skills your child studied on the previous pages.

1. Make word cards for your child's bedroom. Tape or pin the words on the objects so your child can begin to learn the words (such as chair, pillow, bed, game, and doll).
2. Have your child say the numbers 1-50 aloud. Have them raise their hand when they say the even numbers, tap the table with the 10's, and stand up with the 5's.

Chapter 50

Today's lesson will be lots of fun as we join Bogart and Sam as they forge ahead into the heart of the jungle!

While they explore, you will have a good time learning:
• Word formation
• Numerical sequence

Now let's see what's going on deep within the jungle!

Making Words

Using the picture cues and middle and ending sounds, fill in the missing letter to complete the word.

___ig

___og

___ut

___at

___am

___et

Making Words

Using the picture cues and beginning and middle sounds, fill in the missing letter to complete the word.

su___

sa___

te___

pe___

ca___

fro___

Missing Letters

Fill in the missing letters.

A   B   C   __   E

F   G   __   I   __

__   L   M   N   __

__   Q   R   S   __

U   __   W   X

__   Z

Number Sequencing

Place these numbers in order.

___ ___ ___ ___ ___

___ ___ ___ ___ ___

Write on these lines!

Missing Numbers

Fill in the missing numbers.

1 2 3 __ 5 6 __ 8 9 __

11 12 __ 14 __ 16 17 __ __ 20

21 22 __ __ __ 26 27 28 29 __

31 32 __ 34 __ 36 37 38 39 40

__ 42 __ 44 __ 46 47 48 __ 50

Assessment

Chapter 50 Review

Your child studied how to make words and determine missing letters and numbers in this chapter.

Your child learned:
- • Word identification.
- • Letter sequencing.
- • Number sequencing (50-59).
- • Identification of items missing from a sequence.

Work with your child on the chapter review activities shown below. If your child has difficulty with any of these exercises, go back through the chapter with him or her to review the material. You can also review and reinforce these skills with your child using the exercises in the additional activities section below.

1. Ask your child to complete the words below by using the beginning sounds/letters that are provided.

      b   t   d   s

  ___og   ___ix   ___ed   ___en

2. Have your child complete the words below by using the ending sounds/letters that are provided.

      r   p   u   n

  to___   fo___   te___   yo___

3. Tell your child to fill in the missing number and color words.

    One baseball plus one baseball equals _____ baseballs.

    There is a _____ and _____ bumble bee in the yard.

Additional Activities

Below are some interactive ways you and your child can practice what you have worked on in this chapter. These activities will reinforce the skills your child studied on the previous pages.

1. Say the alphabet, but "hum" a random, missing letter. Have your child identify the missing letter that you replaced with a "hum." Let your child try this with you.
2. Have your child sound out and write the colors of the rainbow and the number words 1-10.

Answer Key

Chapter 1
Answer Key

Assessment Activities—
1. Child should trace the letters.
2. 2, 6, 8.
3. 0, 3, 6, 8

Chapter 2
Answer Key

Page 16 – Color king, key, and kangaroo.

Page 18 – 3, 5, 8, 11, 12, 14, 17, 19.

Page 19 – 8, 10, circle 10. 12, 10, circle 12. 4, 6, circle 6.

Assessment Activities—
1. 0, 1, 2, 3, 4, 5, 6, 7, 8, 9.
2. Answers will vary.
3. 10 umbrellas, 9 sea shells, 8 buckets of sand, 6 suns, and 11 shovels.

Chapter 3
Answer Key

Page 25 – Circle bird, butterfly, bug, and bee.

Page 26 – 13, 20, 15.

Assessment Activities—
1. Draw lines: b – B, a – A, z – Z, y – Y.
2. Draw an X on the cat, dog, and gum.
3. Answers will vary.

Chapter 4
Answer Key

Page 30 – Draw a line from the drum to the duck, doll, dolphin, deer, and finally the date tree.

Page 32 – 14 red balls, 9 blue dolphins, 17 green blankets.

Page 33 – 4 blue caps, 2 black socks, 1 yellow book, 2 purple pencils.

Assessment Activities—
1. Answers will vary.
2. Horse, goat, rock.
3. 5,1.

Answer Key

Chapter 5
Answer Key

Page 37 – Circle frog, flamingo, feather, and flower.

Page 39 – 12, 4, 9, 20, and 14.

Page 40 – 4, 7, 18, 3, and 10.

Assessment Activities—

1. L – log. T – tree.
2. 11, 14, 12.
3. 11, 14, 15, 17, 19.

Chapter 6
Answer Key

Page 44 – Hand: circle yes. Bike: circle no. Table: circle no. Hen: circle yes. Bug: circle no. House: circle yes. Heart: circle yes.

Page 46 – Draw lines to the jack in the box, jar, jeep, and jet.

Page 47 – Circle 7, 8, 9. Circle 18, 19, 20. Circle 10, 11, 12. Circle 13, 14, 15.

Assessment Activities—

1. 8,10; 13,15; 7,9; 17,19.
2. Draw lines to J from the jar, jam, and jeep. Draw lines to the H from the house, hammer and ham.

Chapter 7
Answer Key

Page 51 – Draw a line from mitten, money, mouse, mug, and mop.

Page 52 – Circle nest, necklace, nail, and nut.

Page 53 – Draw a line from cap to mop. Draw a line from bat to hat. Draw a line from pad to rod.

Page 54 – Draw a line from 34 to 35 to 36 to 37 to 33. A star.

Assessment Activities—

1. n, t, t, t, n.
2. 24, 29, 32, 38, 40.

Answer Key

Chapter 8
Answer Key

Page 58 – Draw an X on carrot, cookie, and sandwich.

Page 59 – Draw a line from 11 to the sand castles. Draw a line from 12 to sand shovels. Draw a line from 13 to towels. Draw a line from 14 to sand pails. Draw a line from 15 to chairs.

Page 60 – 12: add 2 boats. 16: add 5. 17: draw 13. 20: draw 6.

Page 61 – Draw 11 shovels, draw 8 pails, draw 14 raindrops.

Assessment Activities—

1. Answers will vary.

2. 14 birds, 14 shovels, 11 suns, 12 pails, and 13 shells.

3. Answers will vary.

Chapter 9
Answer Key

Page 65 – Circle rain, rainbow, rat, raft, rose, and rock.

Page 66 – Draw 6 girls and 5 boys.

Page 67 – Draw from five to 5 to the 5 balls. Draw a line from nine to 9 to the 9 balls. Draw a line from twelve to 12 to the 12 balls. Draw line from three to 3 to the three balls.

Page 68 – Draw a line from 1 star to 2 stars to 3 stars to 4 stars to 5 stars to 6 stars to 7 stars to 8 stars to 9 stars to 10 stars.

Assessment Activities—

1. Three OOO, Five OOOOO, Nine OOOOOOOOO.

2. 11: right. 12: middle. 13: left. 14: middle.

3. Answers will vary.

Chapter 10
Answer Key

Page 72 – Draw a line to connect the sink, sun, skunk, and soap.

Page 73 – Color the tiger, tent, tire, table, and toothbrush.

Page 74 – 14, 9. Circle 9.

10, 15. Circle 10.

3, 2. Circle 2.

Assessment Activities—

1. Circle turtle and tree. Draw an X on the sandwich and star.

2. Answers will vary.

3. Child should draw 4 birds, 6 pencils, and 10 stars.

Answer Key

Chapter 11
Answer Key

Page 78 – Circle L. Circle M.

Page 79 – Draw a line from eleven to 11. Draw a line from twelve to 12. Draw a line from fourteen to 14. Draw a line from thirteen to 13.

Page 80 – 30, 40, 50, 60, 70, 80, 90, and 100.

Page 81 – Circle 10 pandas, 10 cars, 10 frogs, 10 yo-yos, and 10 dolls.

Assessment Activities—

    1. D, F, G, J, and L.

    2. 15, 12, 13, and 11.

    3. 40, 60, 80, and 90.

Chapter 12
Answer Key

Page 84 – U, X, and Z.

Page 85 – B, L, V, O, and F.

Page 86 – d, g, i, and l.

Page 87 – 1, 2, 6, 5, and 4.

Page 88 – MITTEN.

Assessment Activities—

    1. B, E, I, K, L, and N.

    2. 2, 3, and 5.

    3. TEETH.

Chapter 13
Answer Key

Page 91 – Letters should be connected as follows: k, l, m, n, o, p, q, r, s, t.

Page 92 – e, g, j, m.

Page 93 – 4, 2, 3.

Page 94 – 7 students like reading best. 3 students like writing. 9 students like art.

Assessment Activities—

    1. O, Q, U.

    3. Answers will vary.

Answer Key

Chapter 14
Answer Key

Page 97 – Letters should be connected in ABC order, begining with A and ending with Z.

Page 98 – 2: **b**at. 3: **c**at. 4: **d**og. 5: **e**gg.

Page 99 – 2: **m**ice. 3: **n**est. 4: **o**wl. 5: **p**ig.

Page 100 – There are corn stalks in the right foreground. The truck in the upper left is purple, not blue. The sheep in the upper right are white, not brown.

Page 101 – There is a sun in the background behind the barn. There is a rabbit next to the tractor. The turtle is facing the opposite direction. There are extra flowers in the left foreground. There is no steam coming out of the tractor.

Assessment Activities—

1. R, D, G, J, N.

2. **J**ar, **K**ite, **L**ion, **M**ice.

Chapter 15
Answer Key

Page 104 – Map, mitt.

Page 105 – Circle the "r" at the beginning of rat and rod.

Page 106 – 2: C. 3: E.

Page 107 – 3 blue pens, 6 paper clips, 2 red pens, 5 smiley faces, 1 pencil, 2 erasers, and 4 rubber bands.

Page 108 – 3 blue squares, 4 orange triangles, 2 green circles, 1 red trapezoid, and 5 purple rectangles.

Assessment Activities—

1. Milk, mouse.

2. Circle the "b" in ball and bat.

Chapter 16
Answer Key

Page 111 – Bed – bat. Key – king. Ring – raccoon.

Page 112 – Sun and Sam.

Page 113 – Sun – sock. Pin – pot. Net – nail.

Page 114 – 6 small shapes, 5 large shapes, 5 medium shapes.

Page 115 – Color one of each in blue, red, and green: Leaf, face, rock, hut, bird.

Assessment Activities—

1. Kite – key. Pear – pineapple. Hat – horn. Balloon – bed.

2. Circle 6 small shapes and 6 large shapes.

Answer Key

Chapter 17
Answer Key

Page 118 – Sun, six, sad, and sock.

Page 119 – Sun.

Page 120 – 2: 1 + 2 = 3. 3: 0 + 1 = 1. 4: 3 + 0 = 3.

Page 121 – Color + stars red and - stars blue.

Page 122 – There are 11 red plus signs and 8 blue minus signs.

Assessment Activities—

1. Cake, cat, and call should be marked with X's.

2. Happy should be circled.

3. The drawing: 4 red balloons, 2 blue balloons.

   The number sentence: 4 + 2 = 6.

Chapter 18
Answer Key

Page 125 – Color the car.

Page 126 – First row – pen. Second row – map. Third row – leaf.

Page 127 – Block, banana, ball, and bee should be colored.

   Shell and ring should be circled.

Page 128 – Step 1 – count 4 birds. Step 2 – count on 5, 6. Sam saw 6 birds.

Page 129 – From the top down: penny, nickel, dime, quarter.

Assessment Activities—

1. The hat should be colored.

2. First row: wall. Second row: hat.

3. The picture should show 2 sets of 2 toy cars. There are 4 cars total.

Answer Key

Chapter 19
Answer Key

Page 132 – Shirt, hat.

Page 133 – Bun, spoon, can, and pan.

Page 134 – Rod, cloud, and sled.

Page 135 – Cloud 2: penny – 1 cent. Cloud 3: nickel – 5 cents.
Cloud 4: quarter – 25 cents.

Page 136 – Penny (1 cent), nickel (5 cents), dime (10 cents).

Assessment Activities—

1. Bat, hat.

2. Hen, tin, spoon.

3. Dime – 10 cents. Nickel – 5 cents. Penny – 1 cent. Quarter – 25 cents.

Chapter 20
Answer Key

Page 139 – Ham, jam, gum, plum, and drum.

Page 140 – Mop, stop, map, top, and lip.

Page 141 – 4:00. 5:00. 6:00. Rosa may play at 6:00.

Page 142 – 11:00, 6:00, 8:00, 5:00.

Page 143 – Hands should be on 12 and 7, 12 and 10, 12 and 9, 12 and 3,
12 and 12.

Page 144 – 7:00 PM, 1:00 AM, 10:00 PM.

Assessment Activities—

1. Drum, arm.

2. Cap, mop, trap, and bump.

3. 1 – 5:00

2 – 2:00

3 – 6:00

Answer Key

Chapter 21
Answer Key

Page 147 – Box, six.

Page 148 – Bug, bag, mug, and dog.

Page 149 – Bee, car, and hat.

Page 150 – 1: 4 inches. 2: 2 inches. 3: 1 inch. An inch worm.

Page 151 – Row 2: 3, 1, 2

Row 3: 2, 3, 1

Assessment Activities—

1. Peg, tag, and leg.

2. Ball, net, and pan.

3. Answers will vary.

Chapter 22
Answer Key

Page 154 – Net, cat.

Page 155 – Hat, cat.

Page 156 – 7 squares should be colored.

Page 157 – 8 triangles.

Page 158 – 7 triangles should be traced.

Assessment Activities—

1. Hat and kite have the same ending sound, even though they end with different letters.

2. 4 triangles.

3. A square has 4 sides. 3 squares should be drawn.

Chapter 23
Answer Key

Page 161 – Rug, dog, and pig.

Page 162 – Fox.

Page 163 – Fish, cat, and grapes.

Page 164 – 5 green squares. 5 red triangles.

Page 165 – Dots are connected from 1 to 25.

Assessment Activities—

1. Pan.

2. Pet, bat, fast.

3. 3.

Answer Key

Chapter 24
Answer Key

Page 170 – There should be 7 circles crossed out.

Page 171 – There are 6 rectangles.

Page 172 – There are 8 purple circles and 6 yellow rectangles.

Assessment Activities—

1. Draw a line from cat to bat to hat. Draw a line from frog to log to dog.

2. Answers will vary.

3. 8 circles. 6 rectangles.

Chapter 25
Answer Key

Page 175 – Color hat, mat, and sat.

Page 176 – Hop, top, pop. Yes, the words rhyme.

Page 177 – The largest trapezoid (on the far right).

Page 178 – From top to bottom: trapezoid, circle, hexagon, triangle, octagon, and rectangle.

Page 179 – Octagon and triangle. Circle and hexagon. Triangle and rectangle.

Assessment Activities—

1. og, ox, at.

2. There should be 2 blue hexagons and 2 purple trapezoids. Rectangles and circles should be left blank.

3. Octagon. Rectangle and circles. Circles and rectangles.

Chapter 26
Answer Key

Page 182 – Circle dot, and cot.

Page 183 – Pup. Cup. Yes, they rhyme.

Page 184 – Circle sun, bun, and run.

Page 185 – 7 circle, circle, square patterns should be colored.

Assessment Activities—

1. Wet, get, set, bet.

2.

3. Answers will vary.

Answer Key

Chapter 27
Answer Key
Page 190 – "The" should be circle 5 times.

Page 191-2 – First and Fourth tree should be one color. Other trees should be a different color. Monkeys should be one color. Bananas should be a different color.

Page 193 – **The** cat ran away from **the** dog.

Assessment Activities—

1. **The** cat and **the** dog and **the** boy went to **the** lake to catch **the** fish.

2.

3. **the** dog. **the** cat. **the** mom. **the** dad.

Chapter 28
Answer Key
Page 196 – It is my car. It is red. It is fun.

Page 197 – Blue dog, green fox, purple cat, yellow bat.

Assessment Activities—

1. is, is, and is. Answers will vary.

2. Red, yellow, blue.

3.

Chapter 29
Answer Key
Page 203 – Sled, snowman, pine trees, hat.

Page 204 – Watering can, bird.

Page 205 – No, yes, yes, yes.

Page 206 – Jeep, Shoe, person.

Page 207 – Flower.

Assessment Activities—

1. The first and third pair of numbers.

2. Chair, book, car.

3. A star above the 2s.

Answer Key

Chapter 30
Answer Key

Page 211 – Birds and Fish. Snakes and Turtles. Lizards and Frogs.

Page 212 – Meg, Kip, Tom, Pat, Tim, and Ned.

Page 213 – Seal, penguin, polar bear.

Page 214 – The penguin.

Assessment Activities—

1. Circle "I" and "and" in the first sentence. Circle "a" in the second.
2. Circle the third pair of numbers.
3. East.

Chapter 31
Answer Key

Page 217 – My twig, my flower, my rock.

Page 220 – Blue/Left – Hat. Red/Right – Ball.

Page 221 – Left/red – fox.

       Above/blue – snow cloud.

       Right/yellow – snow boots.

       Below/orange – South Pole.

Assessment Activities—

1. Circle "is." Block "my."
2. Write "my" in each blank.
3. Circle "is" in each sentence.

Chapter 32
Answer Key

Page 227 – Circle second, fifth, and sixth arrows.

Page 228 – **I** am going to **a** new school.

Assessment Activities—

1. **I** put **a** bug in the box.

Answer Key

Chapter 33
Answer Key

Page 231 – A, E, F, H, I, K, L, M, N, T, V, W, X, Y, Z.

Page 232 – A, E, F, H, I, K, L, M, N, T, V, W, X, Y, Z.

Page 233 – Answers may vary.

Page 234 – Shoes, socks, mittens.

Page 235 – Draw one of each: eye, shoe, mitten, hand, sock.

Assessment Activities—

    1. Z, A, K.

    2. Ears, shoes, mittens.

Chapter 34
Answer Key

Page 238 – B, D, G, J, P, Q, R.

Page 239 – B, R, O, Q, S, C, D, G, J, P, U.

Page 240 – Answers may vary.

Page 248 – Girl without a soccer ball.

Assessment Activities—

    1. A.

    2. S, O, C.

    3. B, R.

Chapter 35
Answer Key

Page 245 – Apple, banana, carrot, doughnut, egg.

Page 248 – Balloons – B

              Frogs – F

              Cats – C

Page 249 – Boy finding his dog.

Assessment Activities—

    1. A, B, C, D, E.

    2. Banana – B. Apple – A. Carrot – C.

Answer Key

Chapter 36

Answer Key

Page 253 – H – hammer. I – ice cream. K – kites.

Page 254 – Say is, I, and, in, cat, it, can, arm, sat, man, ran, hat, man, an, if.

Page 255 – One – tree. Two – flowers. Three – children. Four – footballs. Five – dogs.

Page 256 – Write three, five, two, three, four.

Assessment Activities—

1. it, is, if, in.

2. One, two, three, four, five.

3. S – 6. T – 2. F – 5. N – 9.

Chapter 37

Answer Key

Page 260 – N – noses. P – popcorn. R – robot.

Page 261 – Write I, and, the. Use sign language.

Page 262 – six: zebra, seven: elephants, eight: balloons, nine: snakes; ten: goats.

Page 263 – six: bees; seven: flowers. eight: butterflies. nine: bats. ten: lizards.

Assessment Activities—

1. Not, octopus, parrot, quack.

2. Not, Sam, an, of.

3. Six, three, nine, four, two.

Chapter 38

Answer Key

Page 268 – Write at, is, in, and sign the words.

Page 269 – In, is, at.

Page 270 – 20, 21, 22, 23, 24, 25.

Page 271 – 20, 21, 22, 23, 24, 25.

Assessment Activities—

1. 1, 2, 3, 4, 5, 6, 7, 8, 9, 10, 11, 12, 13, 14, 15, 16, 17, 18, 19, 20.

2. Fat, mat, cat, sat.

3. 15, 16, **17**, **18**, 19, **20**, 21, 22, **23**, 24, **25**, **26**, **27**, 28, 29, 30.

Answer Key

Chapter 39
Answer Key

Page 277 – 10-cent item and 25-cent item.

Page 278 – Quarter – 25 cents

Nickel – 5 cents

Dime – 10 cents

Penny – 1 cent

Assessment Activities—

1. Answers will vary.

Chapter 40
Answer Key

Page 281 – Bat, cat, sat, fat, mat, hat.

Page 282 – Fit, hit, pit, sit.

Page 284 – 2 Js, 2 Os, 1 E, 1 H, 1 N, 1 S, 2 As, 2 Ms, 2 Ts, Matt.

Assessment Activities—

1. Bat, cat, hat.

Hit, sit, bit.

3. S –1. A – 3. M – 2. R –2. K – 1. Y –1. "A" appears most often.

Chapter 41
Answer Key

Page 288 – Ham, jam, Pam, Sam.

Page 289 – Fin, pin, tin, win.

Page 290 – 2, 5, 4, 3, 1.

Assessment Activities—

1. Pam, ham, jam. Win, pin, fin.

2. Fourth **4**, Second **2**, First **1**, Third **3**, Fifth **5**.

3. Circle the fox. Put an X over the dog and a box around the frog.

Answer Key

Chapter 42
Answer Key

Page 296 – Answers will vary.

Page 297 – Can, fan, man, pan, tan, van.

Page 298 – 80, **81**, **82**, 83, 84, 85, **86**, 87, 88, **89**.

Page 299 – 11, 12, 13, 14, 15, 16. 25, 26, 27, 28, 29, 30.

Assessment Activities—

    1. 8, 17, 22, 43, 60.

    2. an = fan, tan, pan. at = cat, bat, sat.

    3. 11, 25, 58, 87.

Chapter 43
Answer Key

Page 302 – Circle: Stop – top. Sky – butterfly. Mocha – tapioca. Underline: Green, red, yellow, brown, blue, yellow, mocha, white, black, pink, mocha, yellow.

Page 303 – 50, 51, 52, 53, 54, 55 56, 57, 58, 59, 60.

Page 304 – 3.

Page 305 – 9.

Page 306 – 15.

Assessment Activities—

    1. Coat/boat, hat/cat, shoe/blue, log/dog.

    2. Words that rhyme with cat, go, red, and top.

    3. 11, 99.

Chapter 44
Answer Key

Page 309 – Two shoe, four door, six sticks, eight straight, ten hen. One, two, three, four, five, six, seven, eight, nine, ten.

Page 311 – Carrot, Nose.

Page 312 – Robot, Ring.

Page 313 – Popcorn, Flower.

Page 314 – 4, 5, 6, 7, 8, 9. 11, 12, 13, 14, 15, 16.

Assessment Activities—

    1. Write words that rhyme with it, at, is, and in.

    2. Cat/fat. Top/stop. Run/fun. Red/bed.

    3. Square, x, square, x, square.

       #, #, 1, #, #.

       2, 4, 2, 4, 2, 4, 2, 4.

Answer Key

Chapter 45
Answer Key
Page 317 – Bat, cat, fat, hat, mat, pat, rat, and sat. (Order of answers will vary).

Page 318 – Pictures will vary.

Page 320 – 0, 2, 4, 6, 8, 10 ,12, 14, 16, 18, 20.

Page 321 – 30, 31, 32, 33, 34, 35, 36, 37, 38, 39.

Assessment Activities—

    1. 2, 4, 6, 8, 10 ,12, 14, 16, 18, and 20.

    2. 2, 4, 6, 8, 10, 16.

    3. Answers will vary but could include: Bat, cat, fat, hat, mat, pat, rat, or sat.

Chapter 46
Answer Key
Page 324 – It, in, is, if.

Page 325 – At, an, as, am.

Page 326 – 1 line, 4 square, 3 triangle, 8 octagon.

Page 327 – 40, 41, 42, 43, 44, 45, 46, 47, 48, and 49.

Page 328 – 1 unicycle, 2 bike, 4 jeep, 4 car.

Assessment Activities—

    1. Circle = most. Heart = least.

    2. Answers may vary, but could include fin, win, and tin. Sit, bit, and fit.

Chapter 47
Answer Key
Page 331 – Stop/start; Up/Down; On/off.

Page 332 – He caught the butterfly.

Page 333 – She chose a turtle.

Page 334 – 70, 71, 72, 73, 74, 75, 76, 77, 78, and 79.

Page 335 – Winter clothing : 3 (mittens, hat, and boots). Summer clothing: 2 (shorts and sunglasses).

Assessment Activities—

    1. Ladybug.

    2. Graph should show 5 red apples, 3 yellow apples and 1 green apple.

Answer Key

Chapter 48
Answer Key

Page 338 – Fill in the letters and glue pictures to the boxes. Cut out all boxes.

Page 339 – Fill in the letters and glue pictures to the boxes. Cut out all boxes.

Page 340 – 90, 91, 92, 93, 94, 95, 96, 97, 98, and 99.

Page 342 – 10, 20, 30, 40, and 50 (not: 0, 5, 11, 15, 16, 25, 36, and 47).

Assessment Activities—

    1. A, D, G, J, L, N.

Chapter 49
Answer Key

Page 345 – Fill in the letters and glue pictures to the boxes. Cut out all boxes.

Page 346 – Fill in the letters and glue pictures to the boxes. Cut out all boxes.

Page 347 – 60, 61, 62, 63, 64, 65, 67, 68, 69.

Page 348 – Play Bingo.

Assessment Activities—

    1. B, G, L, P, S, V, and Z.

    2. 1, 6, 11, 16, 20, 29, 34, 43, 50.

    3. Cat, fin, stop, top, van.

Chapter 50
Answer Key

Page 352 – Pig, log, nut, hat, ham, and net.

Page 353 – Sun, sad, ten, pen, cat, and frog.

Page 354 – D, H, J, K, O, P, T, V, and Y.

Page 355 – 50, 51, 52, 53, 54, 55, 56, 57, 58, and 59.

Page 356 – 4, 7, 10, 13, 15, 18, 19, 23, 24, 25, 30, 33, 35, 41, 43, 45, 49.

Assessment Activities—

    1. Dog, six, bed, and ten.

    2. Top, for, ten, and you.

    3. Two, black, yellow.

Use these pages to practice writing letters and numbers.

Use these pages to practice writing letters and numbers.

Use these pages to practice writing letters and numbers.

Use these pages to practice writing letters and numbers.

Use these pages to practice writing letters and numbers.

Use these pages to practice writing letters and numbers.

Use these pages to practice writing letters and numbers.

Use these pages to practice writing letters and numbers.

Use these pages to practice writing letters and numbers.

Use these pages to practice writing letters and numbers.

This page has been provided for use with the assessment pages at the end of each chapter.

This page has been provided for use with the assessment pages at the end of each chapter.

This page has been provided for use with the assessment pages at the end of each chapter.

This page has been provided for use with the assessment pages at the end of each chapter.

This page has been provided for use with the assessment pages at the end of each chapter.

This page has been provided for use with the assessment pages at the end of each chapter.